THE NEWEST DASH MINI WAFFLE MAKER COOKBOOK

1500 Days Delicious, and Healthy DASH Mini Waffle Maker Recipes

Copyright©2023 Britney R. Bruner

All rights reserved. No part of this book may be reproduced

or used in any manner without the prior written permission

of the copyright owner, except for the use of brief quotations

in a book review.

Printed by Amazon in the USA.

Disclaimer : Although the author and publisher have made every effort to ensure that the information in this book was correct at press time, the author and publisher do not assume and hereby disclaim any liability to any party for any loss, damage, or disruption caused by errors or omissions, whether such errors or omissions result from negligence, accident, or any other cause. this book is not intended as a substitute for the medical advice of physicians.

TABLE OF CONTENTS

INTRODUCTION **6**

KETO CHAFFLES RECIPES **15**

Pumpkin Spice Keto Waffle 15

Keto "apple" Fritter Chaffles 15

Keto Smores Chaffle 16

Keto Chocolate Twinkie Copycat Chaffle Recipe 17

Keto Chaffle Stuffing Recipe 17

Keto Taco Chaffle Recipe 18

Keto Eggs Benedict 19

Cinnamon Roll Keto Chaffles 20

Keto Sausage Ball Chaffle Recipe 21

Keto Low Carb Cinnamon Roll Chaffles 21

Strawberries & Cream Keto Chaffles 22

Keto Taco Chaffle Recipe 23

Quick & Easy Keto Sausage Gravy Recipe 23

Keto Chocolate Chip Chaffle Keto Recipe 24

Keto Chaffle Glazed Donut 24

Keto Chaffle Churro Recipe 25

Keto Chaffle Garlic Cheesy Bread Sticks 25

Keto Pumpkin Chaffles 26

Keto Oreo Chaffles 26

Pumpkin Chaffle Keto Sugar Cookies 27

Keto Wookie Cookie Recipe 28

The Best Keto Tuna Melt Chaffle Recipe 28

How To Make A Keto Taco Salad Bowl 29

Nut-free Keto Cinnamon Roll Chaffles 29

Keto Big Mac Recipe With Homemade Keto Big Mac Sauce 31

Keto Lemon Chaffle Recipe 32

Keto Vanilla Twinkie Copycat Chaffle Recipe 32

Keto Chocolate Chaffle Recipe 33

Keto Rye Bread Chaffle Recipe 33

Sausage Egg And Cheese Keto Copycat Mcgriddle Recipe 34

Keto Parmesan Garlic Chaffles - 3 Ways 34

Keto Chaffle Recipe 35

Keto Strawberry Shortcake Chaffles 35

Keto Cauliflower Chaffles Recipe 36

Keto Cornbread Chaffle Recipe 37

Keto Pizza Chaffle Recipe 38

New & Improved Keto Waffles 38

Easy Keto Peanut Butter Chaffles 39

The Best 3 Ingredient Keto Waffles 39

Easy Keto Pizza Chaffles 40

Keto Pumpkin Chaffle Cake 40

Keto Chaffle Blt Sandwich 41

CHAFFLE CAKE RECIPES 42

Tiramisu Chaffle Cake Recipe 42

Keto Strawberry Cake Chaffle Recipe 42

Keto Chocolate Waffle Cake Recipe 43

Keto Red Velvet Waffle Cake Recipe 44

Strawberry Shortcake Chaffle Recipe 44

Banana Pudding Chaffle Cake 45

Coconut Cream Cake Chaffle Recipe 45

Keto Boston Cream Pie Chaffle Cake Recipe 46

Chocolate Chip Cookie Chaffle Cake Recipe 47

Strawberry Shortcake Chaffles 48

Keto Birthday Cake Chaffle Recipe 49

Keto Italian Cream Chaffle Cake Recipe 49

Keto Peanut Butter Chaffle Cake Recipe 50

Easy Soft Cinnamon Rolls Chaffle Cake 51

Lemon Cake Chaffles 51

Almond Joy Cake Chaffle Recipe 52

Pecan Pie Chaffle Cake 53

Carrot Chaffle Cake Recipe 53

Cap'n Crunch Cereal Chaffle Cake 54

German Chocolate Chaffle Cake Recipe 55

Halloween Monster Chocolate Chaffle Cake Recipe ..56

BREAKFAST CHAFFLES RECIPES 57

Keto Blt Chaffle Sandwich 57

Open-faced Keto French Dip Sandwich With A Chaffle 57

Halloween Spiced Ghost Pancakes Recipe 58

Garlic Bread Chaffle 59

Jicama Hash Brown Chaffle Recipe 59

Easy Corndog Chaffle Recipe 60

Avocado Toast Chaffle Recipe 60

Low Carb Reuben Chaffle Sandwich Recipe 61

Easy Turkey Burger With Halloumi Cheese Chaffle Recipe 61

Keto Fluffernutter Sandwich Recipe 61

Chocolate Chip Cannoli Chaffle Recipe 63

Zucchini Nut Bread Chaffle Recipe 63

Jalapeno Popper Grilled Cheese Chaffle Recipe 64

Okra Fritter Chaffles Recipe 64

Big Mac Chaffle 65

Taco Chaffle Recipe 66

Apple Pie Churro Chaffle Tacos Recipe 67

Chickfila Copycat Chaffle Sandwich Recipe 68

Dairy Free And Egg Free Chaffle Bread Recipe 68

Dill Pickle Egg Salad Sandwiches 69

Gingerbread Chaffles 69

Keto Sweet Bread Chaffle Recipe 70

Cheesy Garlic Bread Chaffle Recipe 70

Fried Pickle Chaffle Sticks 71

Keto Wonder Bread Chaffle Recipe 71

Corndog Chaffle Recipe 72

SAVORY CHAFFLE RECIPES **73**

Halloumi Cheese Chaffle Recipe 73

Peanut Butter & Jelly Sammich Chaffle Recipe 73

Blueberry & Brie Grilled Cheese Chaffle 73

Everything Bagel Chaffle Recipe 74

Banana Nut Chaffle Recipe 75

Crispy Cheddar Chaffles Recipe 75

Cranberry Swirl Chaffles With Orange Cream Cheese Frosting 76

Everything Bagel Chaffles 77

Jicama Loaded Baked Potato Chaffle 77

Biscuits And Gravy Chaffle Recipe 78

The Best Chaffle Recipe 78

Peppermint Mocha Chaffles With Buttercream Frosting 80

Key Lime Pie Chaffle Recipe 80

Rice Krispie Treat Chaffle Copycat Recipe 81

Crispy Everything Bagel Chaffle Chips 81

Chaffle Pizza 82

Peanut Butter Cup Chaffles 83

Apple Pie Fries With Caramel Dipping Sauce Recipe 83

Pizza Chaffles 85

Savory Chaffle 85

Krispy Kreme Copycat Of The Glazed Raspberry Jelly-filled Donut 86

Pumpkin Spice Chaffles 86

Carnivore Chaffle Recipe 87

SWEET CHAFFLE RECIPES **88**

Pumpkin Pie Chaffle 88

Pumpkin Chaffle With Cream Cheese Frosting Recipe 88

Chocolate Chip Chaffles 89

Cream Cheese Chaffles 89

Coconut Chocolate Chip Macadamia Nut Chaffles 90

Blueberry Chaffles 90

Grilled Cheese Chaffle 91

Mcgriddle Chaffles 91

Pumpkin Chocolate Chip Chaffles 92

Chocolate Chip Chaffles 92

Easy Double Chocolate Chaffles Recipe 93

Strawberry Shortcake Chaffle 93

Cream Cheese Chaffle With Lemon Curd 94

BASIC CHAFFLE RECIPES **95**

Easy Maple Iced Soft Gingerbread Cookies Chaffle Recipe 95

Chicken Jalapeno Popper Chaffle Recipe 95

Bacon Cheddar Bay Biscuits Chaffle Recipe 96

Low-carb Chocolate Chip Vanilla Chaffles Recipe 96

Arby's Chaffle 97

Buffalo Chicken Chaffle Recipe For Low Carb Waffles 97

Low Carb Bagel 98

Jalapeno Popper Chaffles 99

Sloppy Joe Chaffle Recipe 99

Hot Ham & Cheese Chaffles 100

Easy Blueberry Chaffle Recipe 100

Low Carb Sourdough Copycat Wonder Bread Chaffle Recipe 101

Basic Low Carb And Keto Chaffle 101

Oreo Cookie Chaffle Recipe 102

Monte Cristo Chaffle Crepes Recipe 102

Pumpkin Chaffles 103

Lupin Flour Waffle Recipe 103

Zucchini Chaffles 104

Jamaican Jerk Chicken Chaffle 105

Basic Chaffle Recipe 105

Buffalo Chicken Chaffle Recipe 106

Chaffles Benedict 106

Easy Chicken Parmesan Chaffle Recipe 107

Broccoli And Cheese Chaffle 108

INTRODUCTION

One of the first steps in using your waffle maker is selecting the one that's best for you. There are a wide range of waffle makers available and it's important to know what each of them does so you can find the perfect one for your needs. Some have removable plates, some have adjustable heat settings, others are meant for specific types of batter. Some have individual portions while others produce four or more waffles at once. You should also take into account the size and type of space it will be stored in as well as its cost. Ultimately, it's up to you to decide exactly which features will come in handy and which ones you might not need. But by knowing what they all do, you can make a more informed decision when buying a new one.

Making the perfect batter

The perfect waffle starts with the perfect batter. To get a light, fluffy waffle you'll need to ensure that your batter is not too thick. It should pour like cake batter and not be too liquidy. If you can easily see through the batter, it's too thin and will produce a flat waffle. Conversely, if you can't see through the batter at all, it may be too thick and will produce a dense or chewy waffle. The best way to test the thickness of your batter is to see if you can draw lines in it with your whisk or spoon. If you can't see any lines, then your batter is ready to go!

The best cooking time for your waffles

The cooking time for your waffles varies from waffle maker to waffle maker. The best thing to do is look at the instructions that came with your specific waffle machine and choose the setting that corresponds to your desired doneness. The first thing you'll want to do after preparing the batter is pour it into the hot, greased waffle iron. Close the lid, and allow the appliance to cook for 3-5 minutes or until it beeps or tells you it's done. When cooking a fresh batch of waffles, you may need to grease your waffle iron again. If this happens, let your iron heat up before adding more batter.

The importance of using oil when cooking waffles

If you've ever spent time cooking waffles and wondered why they have that crispy texture, there's one thing you need to know: oil. Waffle makers require a little bit of oil, usually in the form of butter or vegetable oil because it is more fluid than other oils. If you are making your own batter, it's best to use melted butter as regular butter will not work well without adding some additional liquid. Add just enough of this fat so that the waffle maker can cook the batter evenly. This will give you a light, crispy waffle that doesn't stick to the waffle maker and is easy to remove when done. The right amount of oil ensures that your waffles are cooked thoroughly and don't get stuck on the outside because they were too dry when cooking.

How to clean your waffle maker

Clean your waffle maker with a damp cloth and some mild dish soap. First, unplug the appliance from the power source. Next, wipe down the surface of your waffle maker with a damp cloth and some mild dish soap to remove any leftover bits of batter or other foods. Finally, thoroughly dry the appliance with a dish towel before storing it away in a safe place for later use.

How do you make waffles in a waffle maker?

First, it's important to make sure you have the right equipment. If the waffle maker doesn't have grids that are deep enough to hold your batter, then you should look for one that does. Next, you need to know how thick your waffle should be. It should be about 1/2 inch in thickness. Your batter can be too thin or too thick, so if it falls off the grid as soon as you put it on, then your batter is too thin and needs more flour. Try adding some more and see if that fixes the problem. Likewise, if your waffle sticks to the grid as soon as you put it on, then your batter is too thick and has a lot of liquid content in it. You can try adding some more flour or milk to see if that makes a difference in thickness.

How much batter do you put in a waffle maker?

The success of your waffle largely depends on the correct amount of batter. Too much or too little batter will leave you with a mess and a dry, cake-like waffle. The right amount is ¼ cup per serving.

Most waffle makers measure out 1 ½ cups of batter. So if you're cooking for two, use three tablespoons of batter per serving and cook for two minutes, turning halfway through to ensure even cooking. First, pour ¼ cup batter onto hot waffle maker grill. Cook until it starts to brown (2-3 minutes). Then flip over to brown the other side of the waffles (1-2 minutes).

Should I preheat the waffle maker?

One of the first things you will want to do is preheat your waffle maker. This will ensure that it is nice and hot when the batter is poured in. If you don't preheat, it could take up to 15 minutes for your waffles to cook through (and, who has time for that?). To preheat, all you need to do is plug it in and let it heat on medium-high for 3-5 minutes. No need to wait any longer than that. What if I accidentally overcook my waffles? If you end up overcooking your waffles, there are a few easy ways to save them. You can either toast them on a pan or put them in the microwave with some butter and syrup. Whatever works best!

Do you have to put oil on a waffle maker?

Waffle makers are a handy appliance that can make everything from waffles to pancakes in a matter of minutes. And while they're not the most complicated device you may own, there is some information about them that many people are left wondering. One of the most common questions is if you need to put oil on the waffle maker before cooking your food. If you have an uncoated cooking surface (like a non-stick surface), then it's not necessary to put oil on your waffle maker. The reason for this is because any oils will be released from the food and spread across the surface as it cooks. But, if your cooking surface isn't non-stick, then we recommend putting a little bit of oil onto your spatula and rubbing it across the entire surface of your waffle maker before cooking anything on it. This will create an even coating that will prevent food from sticking to your cooking surface!

How do you make waffles not stick to the waffle maker?

One of the most common mistakes people make when cooking waffles is not greasing the waffle maker. When you cook your batter, it will stick to the grates and make it difficult to remove. To avoid this, all you have to do is use a little bit of oil on the grates before cooking your waffles. This ensures that the batter won't stick and makes cleanup a breeze.

A word of caution: If you're making Belgian-style waffles, don't use too much oil or they will end up being crispy instead of fluffy.

How long do I cook waffles in a waffle iron?

Waffles cook for about three to four minutes a side in a standard waffle iron. If you're cooking frozen waffles, you'll need to add an extra minute or two on each side

Should I spray waffle iron?

You might be wondering if you should spray your waffle maker before making waffles. The answer is almost always "yes." Some waffle makers have non-stick coatings and won't need to be sprayed, but most will. If your waffle maker doesn't come with a non-stick coating, don't worry! You'll just need to grease it using some coconut oil or butter. Spray the inside of the plates with cooking spray or grease them with butter or oil before pouring in your batter for best results. Remember, you want the grease to coat the entire surface of the plates so that when you pour in your batter, it doesn't stick to any one area. Spraying your plates also prevents any type of outside element from coming into contact with your hot waffle maker, which could possibly harm it. This is especially critical if you're using an old model that is not coated in non-stick material.

Why do you need a flip waffle maker?

Nowadays, flip waffles are very popular. They cook faster than ordinary waffles and they're easier to turn out without messing up the batter.

What setting do you put a waffle maker on?

It's important to know what setting you need to put your waffle maker on. If you set it too high, your waffles will end up burnt and crispy. If you set it too low, they won't cook all the way through. That's why it's a good idea to check the instructions that came with your waffle maker.

How do I know when my waffle maker is done?

One of the most common issues with waffles is that they get stuck in the waffle maker. This is usually because you didn't give your waffle enough time to cook. One way to tell is by looking at the light on your waffle maker. If it's green, then your waffle has cooked for long enough and you can remove it from the machine without a problem. If it's red, then it needs more time and you should wait before removing it from the appliance.

How do you use a handheld waffle iron?

If you've never used a waffle maker before and want to get started, the first thing you need to know is how to use a handheld waffle iron. The most important part of using a handheld waffle iron is ensuring that the batter is only slightly thicker than water. This will allow your waffles to cook evenly on both sides. But what happens if you have too thick of batter? If your batter is too thick, then your waffles won't be able to cook properly and will take longer than necessary to cook through.

How do you know when a dash waffle maker is done?

When you're cooking waffles, it can be hard to tell if they are done. You might think they are and take them out of the waffle maker only to find that they are still a little doughy on the inside. Nobody likes gooey waffles! But how do you know when your waffle maker is done? One way to know for sure is to keep a close eye on the timer. When the timer goes off, open up your maker and check one of your waffles. If it seems like it's ready, then congratulations! Take your waffle out and wait for it to cool before eating it. Another way to test if your waffles are done is by using a fork or a wooden spoon. Stick one into the middle of a waffle and see if it comes out clean with no batter on it. If not, leave them in for another 1-2 minutes until they seem firm enough in the middle. If you do this often enough, you will soon find out what time frame works best for you!

How do you use a dash waffle?

A waffle maker is a handy appliance that makes all your favorite breakfast favorites in just minutes. But you've seen them sitting there for months on end, untouched, and with no one to show you how to use it. Fear not! This step-by-step guide will show you how to use your waffle maker and make some delicious breakfasts. From picking out the perfect waffle maker to knowing if your batter is too thick, this guide covers everything you need to know about making perfect waffles from start to finish. So what are you waiting for? Scroll below and make breakfast like a pro! One of the most popular ways people enjoy their waffles is by cooking them in their waffle maker. If this sounds like something that interests you, we'd love to help! This guide will walk you through every step necessary for cooking a tasty waffle in your own kitchen. To get started, all you need is the following:

1) Waffle Maker

2) Egg

3) Flour

4) Sugar

5) Oil or butter (we recommend almond oil or coconut oil)

6) Milk (we recommend almond milk or soy milk)

7) Salt (we recommend sea salt or Himalayan salt).

How long do you cook a waffle in a dash waffle maker?

It depends on what kind of waffle maker you have. For a DASH Waffle Maker, cook the waffles for about 3-4 minutes. Again, it is crucial to follow the instructions that come with your specific waffle maker.

Can you put pancake mix in a waffle maker?

You can put pancake mix in a waffle maker, but it might not turn out well. Pancakes are a thicker batter than waffles and usually have more sugar in them as well. Waffle makers typically have small grids which can only hold so much batter at a time. If you try to put too much thick batter into your waffle maker, it will overflow and make a mess. Pancakes are already thick, so if you want to use your waffle maker for pancakes, you should decrease the amount of baking powder and add more liquid ingredients like milk or eggs to thin it out.

What is the difference between waffle and pancake batter?

The main difference between waffle and pancake batter is that waffle batter can be made in a waffle maker. Pancake batter will only work in a frying pan or griddle. If you want to make waffles in your waffle maker, then you'll need to make waffle batter.

What to add to waffle mix to make it better?

A lot of people don't know what to add to their waffles to make them better. Luckily for you, there are so many ways you can make your waffles more delicious. You could try a different variety of syrup, like maple or blueberry, or even some peanut butter. Adding some fruit is also a good idea. If you're feeling really adventurous, adding some ice cream on top can be fun too. Get creative and experiment with different toppings until you find something that suits your taste buds!

Is pancake and waffle mix the same?

The question of whether or not pancake and waffle mix is the same may be a new one to you. Some people use pancake and waffle mix interchangeably, while others think they are different ingredients. The answer is that they are similar but not the same. Pancakes are mainly made with flour, which gives them their fluffy texture. They also contain more liquid than their waffle counterparts, which makes them softer when cooked. Waffles on the other hand, have a cake-like texture made from baking powder and eggs for leavening purposes. They're also drier and denser than pancakes and are typically made without sugar or syrup to keep them crisp on both sides.

Can you use water instead of milk to make waffles?

You can use any type of liquid in your waffle batter. But if you want a crispy waffle, the milk will help the outside get crispier, while the water will make it flatter and more moist. If you don't have milk and need to whip up a batch quickly, water is your best bet. The waffles will have a different taste than traditional waffles but they will still be delicious!

Are waffles healthier than pancakes?

You've probably seen ads for low carb diets that include waffles as one of the recommended breakfast options. But are waffles actually better for you than pancakes? It turns out that there is a difference between flour-based waffles and pancake batter. Pancakes are made from a batter that includes milk, water, butter, eggs and baking powder while waffle batter usually just has flour, baking powder and sugar. Waffle batter is also thicker to allow it to rise when cooking whereas pancake batter is more liquidy. So, what does this all mean? It means that while both are healthier than toast or cereals, so you can choose whichever breakfast food sounds the best to you!

Can I use Bisquick Shake n Pour for waffles?

Are you looking for a quick and easy way to make waffles? Look no further than Bisquick Shake n Pour. This product is designed to make a family of four waffles in just minutes and with the addition of eggs, butter, water, and oil. But can they be made into delicious waffles? The answer is yes! Bisquick Shake n Pour is an excellent option for those who are looking for an easy way to make breakfast quickly. But it isn't just for breakfast; this product can also be used as pancake mix or biscuit dough.

Is pancake and waffle mix the same as Bisquick?

No! Pancake and waffle mix is not the same as Bisquick. They may be similar, but they have different proportions of ingredients that make them work differently. Some pancake mixes can also be used in a waffle maker, but make sure you follow the package directions for best results.

Can you use water instead of milk for Bisquick waffles?

When making Bisquick waffles, you can use water instead of milk. The Bisquick mix is dependant on a liquid to make the batter moist, so using either will work. If you have an allergy or preference for one over the other, go with that one.

Can you make Bisquick waffle batter the night before?

There are two types of waffles, yeast and baking powder. Yeast waffles are the ones you buy from the grocery store, which need time to rise. Baking powder waffles use baking powder instead of yeast and don't require rising time, but they are denser in texture. You can make Bisquick waffle batter the night before by preparing your dry ingredients in a bowl and stirring them together. Cover with plastic wrap and place in the refrigerator overnight. In the morning, separate eggs, beat egg whites until stiff peaks form, add beaten egg yolks to dry ingredients, stir until combined then fold in beaten egg whites. Cook as usual for perfect waffles.

Can I freeze waffle batter?

You can freeze waffles, but the texture doesn't come out as crisp.

This is because of the increase in volume that occurs when you freeze food. When you freeze food without air, it expands and becomes thicker. This is what causes the texture to change in different ways. Freezing waffles does not affect the nutritional value or taste of the waffles – if anything, it could actually prolong the freshness and crispiness of your waffles. It is best to make fresh waffles every time and store them in an airtight container or baggie for up to 5 days. If you want to freeze them, then do so before they are fully cooked as we mentioned before. Put them on a cookie sheet lined with parchment paper or wax paper and place them in the freezer until they're frozen solid which should take about 3-5 hours.

KETO CHAFFLES RECIPES

Pumpkin Spice Keto Waffle

Servings:1

Ingredients:

- 1 egg
- 1 oz cream cheese
- 2 tablespoons pumpkin puree
- 1 tablespoon coconut flour
- 2 teaspoons sugar-free sweetener
- ½ teaspoon vanilla
- ¼ teaspoon baking powder
- ⅛ teaspoon pumpkin pie spice
- pinch of salt

Directions:

1. Preheat
2. Preheat waffle maker to medium high heat.
3. Whisk it
4. Whisk together all of the ingredients.
5. Pour it
6. Pour pumpkin chaffle batter into the center of the waffle iron. Close the waffle maker and let cook for 3-5 minutes or until waffle is golden brown and set. If using a mini waffle maker, only pour in half the batter.
7. Remove & serve
8. Remove chaffle from the waffle maker and serve.

Keto "apple" Fritter Chaffles

Servings:4

Ingredients:

- "Apple" Fritter Filling Ingredients:
- 2 cups diced jicama
- 1/4 cup plus 1 tablespoon Swerve sweetener blend
- 4 tablespoons butter
- 1 teaspoon cinnamon
- 1/8 teaspoon nutmeg
- Dash ground cloves
- 1/2 teaspoon vanilla
- 20 drops Lorann Oils apple flavoring
- Chaffle Ingredients:
- 2 eggs
- 1/2 cup grated mozzarella cheese
- 1 tablespoon almond flour
- 1 teaspoon coconut flour
- 1/2 teaspoon baking powder
- Glaze Ingredients:
- 1 tablespoon butter
- 2 teaspoons heavy cream
- 3 tablespoons powdered sweetener
- 1/4 teaspoon vanilla extract

Directions:

1. Keto "Apple" Fritter Chaffle Filling Directions:
2. Peel the jicama and cut into small dice.

3. In a medium skillet over medium-low heat, melt the butter and add the diced jicama and sweetener.

4. Let simmer slowly for 10-20 minutes until the jicama is soft, stirring often. Do not use high heat or the sweetener will caramelize quickly and burn. It should develop a light amber color and will thicken.

5. When the jicama is soft, remove from heat and stir in the spices and flavorings.

6. Keto "Apple" Fritter Chaffle Directions:

7. Preheat waffle iron until hot.

8. In a medium bowl, beat all ingredients, except cheese. Stir the jicama mixture into the eggs.

9. Place 1 tablespoon grated cheese on that waffle iron.

10. Spoon 2 heaping tablespoons of the egg/jicama mixture into the waffle iron and top with another tablespoon cheese.

11. Close the waffle maker and cook 5-7 minutes until nicely browned and crunchy.

12. Remove to a wire rack.

13. Repeat 3-4 times.

14. Keto "Apple" Fritter Chaffle Icing Directions:

15. Melt butter in a small saucepan and add the Swerve and heavy cream.

16. Simmer over medium heat for 5 minutes, or until slightly thickened.

17. Stir in vanilla.

18. Drizzle the hot icing over the chaffles. It will harden as it cools.

Keto Smores Chaffle

Servings:2

Ingredients:

- 1 large Egg
- ½ c. Mozzarella cheese shredded
- ½ tsp Vanilla extract
- 2 tbs Swerve brown
- ½ tbs Psyllium Husk Powder optional
- ¼ tsp Baking Powder
- Pinch of pink salt
- ¼ Lily's Original Dark Chocolate Bar
- 2 tbs Keto Marshmallow Creme Fluff Recipe

Directions:

1. Make the batch of Keto Marshmallow Creme Fluff.

2. Whisk the egg until creamy.

3. Add vanilla and Swerve Brown, mix well.

4. Mix in the shredded cheese and blend.

5. Then add Psyllium Husk Powder, baking powder and salt.

6. Mix until well incorporated, let the batter rest 3-4 minutes.

7. Prep/plug in your waffle maker to preheat.

8. Spread ½ batter on the waffle maker and cook 3-4 minutes.

9. Remove and set on a cooling rack.

10. Cook second half of batter same, then remove to cool.

11. Once cool, assemble the chaffles with the marshmallow fluff and chocolate:

12. Using 2 tbs marshmallow and ¼ bar of Lily's Chocolate.

13. Eat as is, or toast for a melty and gooey Smore sandwich!

Keto Chocolate Twinkie Copycat Chaffle Recipe

Servings:6

Ingredients:

- 2 tablespoons butter melted (cooled)
- 2 ounces cream cheese softened
- 2 large eggs room temp
- 1 tsp vanilla extract
- 1/4 cup Lakanto Confectioners
- Pinch of pink salt
- 1/4 cup almond flour
- 2 tablespoons coconut flour
- 2 tablespoons cacao powder
- 1 teaspoon baking powder

Directions:

1. Preheat the Corndog Maker.

2. Melt the butter and let it cool a minute.

3. Whisk the eggs into the butter until creamy.

4. Add vanilla, sweetener, salt and then blend well.

5. Add Almond flour, coconut flour, cacao powder, and baking powder.

6. Blend until well incorporated.

7. Add ~2 tablespoons batter to each well and spread across evenly.

8. Close lid, lock and let cook 4 minutes.

9. Remove and cool on a rack.

Keto Chaffle Stuffing Recipe

Servings:4

Ingredients:

- Basic Chaffle Ingredients:
- 1/2 cup cheese mozzarella, cheddar or a combo of both
- 2 eggs
- 1/4 tsp garlic powder
- 1/2 tsp onion powder
- 1/2 tsp dried poultry seasoning
- 1/4 tsp salt
- 1/4 tsp pepper
- Stuffing Ingredients:
- 1 small onion diced
- 2 celery stalks
- 4 oz mushrooms diced
- 4 tbs butter for sauteing
- 3 eggs

Directions:

1. First, make your chaffles. This recipe makes 4 mini chaffles.

2. Preheat the mini waffle iron.

3. Preheat the oven to 350F

4. In a medium-size bowl, combine the chaffle ingredients.

5. Pour a 1/4 of the mixture into a mini waffle maker and cook each chaffle for about 4 minutes each.

6. Once they are all cooked, set them aside.

7. In a small frying pan, saute the onion, celery, and mushrooms until they are soft.

8. In a separate bowl, tear up the chaffles into small pieces, add the sauteed veggies and 3 eggs. Mix until the ingredients are fully combined.

9. Add the stuffing mixture to a small casserole dish (about a 4 x 4) and bake it at 350 degrees for about 30 to 40 minutes.

Keto Taco Chaffle Recipe

Ingredients:

- Chaffle Ingredients:
- 1/2 cup cheese cheddar or mozzarella, shredded
- 1 egg
- 1/4 tsp Italian seasoning
- Taco Meat Seasonings Ingredients for 1 lbs of ground beef
- 1 teaspoon chili powder
- 1 teaspoon ground cumin
- 1/2 teaspoon garlic powder
- 1/2 teaspoon cocoa powder
- 1/4 teaspoon onion powder

- 1/4 teaspoon salt
- 1/12 teaspoon smoked paprika
- Taco Meat Seasoning ingredients for Big Batches
- 1/4 cup chili powder
- 1/4 cup ground cumin
- 2 tablespoons garlic powder
- 2 tablespoons cocoa powder
- 1 tablespoon onion powder
- 1 tablespoon salt
- 1 teaspoon smoked paprika

Directions:

1. Cook your ground beef or ground turkey first.

2. Add all the taco meat seasonings. The cocoa powder is optional but it totally enhances the flavors of all the other seasonings!

3. While you are making the taco meat, start making the keto chaffles.

4. Preheat the waffle maker. I use a mini waffle maker.

5. In a small bowl, whip the egg first.

6. Add the shredded cheese and seasoning.

7. Place half the chaffle mixture into the mini waffle maker and cook it for about 3 to 4minutes.

8. Repeat and cook the second half of the mixture to make the second chaffle.

9. Add the warm taco meat to your taco chaffle.

10. Top it with lettuce, tomatoes, cheese, and serve warm!

Keto Eggs Benedict

Servings: 2

Cooking Time: 10 Minutes

Ingredients:

- For the Chaffles
- 2 egg whites
- 2 tbsp almond flour
- 1 tbsp sour cream
- 1/2 cup mozzarella cheese
- For the Hollandaise
- 1/2 cup salted butter
- 4 egg yolks
- 2 tbsp lemon juice
- For the Poached Eggs
- 2 eggs
- 1 tbsp white vinegar
- 3 ounces deli ham

Directions:

1. To prepare the chaffle: Whip the egg white until frothy then blend in the remaining ingredients. Preheat the Dash Mini Waffle Maker and add half the chaffle mixture. Spray the chaffle maker with non-stick cooking spray. Cook about 7 minutes until golden brown. Remove the chaffle and repeat.

2. To prepare the Hollandaise sauce: Assemble a double boiler (a pot with a heat-safe bowl that fits on the top). Put enough water in the pot to boil but so that it doesn't touch the bottom of the bowl.

3. Hollandaise cont: Heat the butter to boiling in the microwave. Add the egg yolks to the bowl of the double boiler and bring the pot to a boil. Add the hot butter to the bowl while the pot comes to a boil.

4. Hollandaise cont: Whisk briskly heating the mixture from the water beneath the bowl. Continue cooking until the water in the pot has boiled, the egg yolk-butter mixture has thickened and is very hot to the touch. Remove the bowl from the pot and add the lemon juice. Set to the side.

5. To poach an egg: Add more water to your pot if necessary (you need enough to completely cover an egg) and bring it to a simmer. Add 2 tbsp of white vinegar to the water. Carefully drop an egg into the simmering water and cook for 90 seconds. Remove with a slotted spoon.

6. To assemble: Warm the chaffle in the toaster for a few minutes. Top the crispy chaffle with half the ham slices, one poached egg, and about 2 tbsp of hollandaise sauce.

7. Enjoy!

Notes

This recipe only uses 4 tbsp of Hollandaise sauce. You'll have some left over. Store it in the fridge and warm it slowly in a double boiler. Do not microwave it or you'll make scrambled eggs.

Cinnamon Roll Keto Chaffles

Servings:3

Cooking Time: 10 Minutes

Ingredients:

- Cinnamon Roll Chaffle Ingredients:
- 1/2 cup mozzarella cheese
- 1 tablespoon almond flour
- 1/4 tsp baking powder
- 1 eggs
- 1 tsp cinnamon
- 1 tsp Granulated Swerve
- Cinnamon roll swirl Ingredients:
- 1 tbsp butter
- 1 tsp cinnamon
- 2 tsp confectioners swerve
- Keto Cinnamon Roll Glaze
- 1 tablespoon butter
- 1 tablespoon cream cheese
- 1/4 tsp vanilla extract
- 2 tsp swerve confectioners

Directions:

1. Cinnamon Roll Chaffles
2. Plug in your Mini Dash Waffle maker and let it heat up.
3. In a small bowl mix the mozzarella cheese, almond flour, baking powder, egg, 1 teaspoon cinnamon and 1 teaspoon swerve granulated and set aside.
4. In another small bowl add a tablespoon of butter, 1 teaspoon cinnamon, and 2 teaspoons of swerve confectioners sweetener.
5. Microwave for 15 seconds and mix well.
6. Spray the waffle maker with non stick spray and add 1/3 of the batter to your waffle maker. Swirl in 1/3 of the cinnamon, swerve and butter mixture onto the top of it. Close the waffle maker and let cook for 3-4 minutes.
7. When the first cinnamon roll chaffle is done, make the second and then make the third.
8. While the third chaffle is cooking place 1 tablespoon butter and 1 tablespoon of cream cheese in a small bowl. Heat in the microwave for 10-15 seconds. Start at 10 and if the cream cheese is not soft enough to mix with the butter heat for an additional 5 seconds.
9. Add the vanilla extract and the swerve confectioners sweetener to the butter and cream cheese and mix well using a whisk.
10. Drizzle keto cream cheese glaze on top of chaffle.

Keto Sausage Ball Chaffle Recipe

Ingredients:

- 1 pound bulk Italian sausage
- 1 cup almond flour
- 2 teaspoons baking powder
- 1 cup sharp cheddar cheese shredded
- 1/4 cup Parmesan cheese grated
- 1 Egg or if you have an egg allergy you can use a Flax Egg (1 T ground flax seed mixed with 3

Directions:

1. Preheat the mini waffle maker.
2. Combine all ingredient in a large mixing bowl and mix well using your hands.
3. Place a paper plate under waffle maker to catch any spillage.
4. Scoop 3 T of mix onto heated waffle maker.
5. Cook for a minimum of 3 minutes. Flip over and cook 2 more minutes for even crispiness.

Keto Low Carb Cinnamon Roll Chaffles

Servings:1

Cooking Time: 2 Minutes

Ingredients:

- 1 egg
- 1/2 cup shredded mozzarella cheese
- 1/2 teaspoon vanilla
- 2 tablespoons Zero Calorie Sweetener
- 1/2 teaspoon ground cinnamon

- Monkfruit Maple Syrup

Directions:

1. Add the egg to a bowl and beat. Add in the remaining ingredients and mix well.
2. Plug in the waffle iron and grease the iron with oil or butter.
3. When hot, add the batter and close the iron.
4. I let my waffles cook until the indicator light on the iron said they were finished. This was about 2 – 2 1/2 minutes. Your timing may vary depending on the iron you use.
5. Carefully remove the waffle from the iron. I like to use a spatula because the waffles are really soft to touch initially.
6. Let the waffles stand for 2-3 minutes. They will firm up.

Notes

Makes 1 large waffle or 2 small waffles.

If you are using a mini waffle iron, divide the batter in half to make 2 waffles.

You may have batter leak out of the waffle iron. This usually happened to me if I tried to evenly spread the batter throughout the iron myself. Focus on spreading it in the middle of the iron and not along the edges. When you close the iron the batter will fill out on its own.

I have tested the recipe using granular sweetener and Confectioner's Sweetener. Both worked fine.

If you do not sweeten chaffles, in my opinion, they taste really savory. I also think that by making them the standard way with just egg and mozzarella, I taste the egg a lot more.

I tested the recipe using 1 tablespoon of sweetener, and felt like the chaffles tasted eggy. Feel free to adjust to your taste and preference.

You can freeze the chaffles. They may soften when you defrost. You can try crisping them in a toaster.

Strawberries & Cream Keto Chaffles

Servings: 8

Cooking Time: 10 Minutes

Ingredients:

- 3 oz cream cheese
- 2 cups mozzarella cheese, shredded
- 2 eggs, beaten
- 1/2 cup almond flour
- 3 tablespoons Swerve confectioners sweetener
- 2 teaspoons baking powder
- 8 strawberries
- 1 cup whipped cream (canister - 2 tablespoons per waffle)
- 1 tablespoon Swerve confectioners sweetener

Directions:

1. Add the cream cheese and mozzarella to a microwavable bowl and cook for 1 minute. Mix well and if all the cheese is melted go to next step. Otherwise cook for 30 seconds more and then mix well.

2. In another bowl, beat eggs then add in the almond flour, baking powder and 3 tablespoons of Swerve sweetener.

3. Add the cream cheese mixture to the almond flour mixture and mix well and then fold in 2 chopped up strawberries. Refrigerate for 20 minutes.

4. In the meantime slice the remaining strawberries and add the 1 tablespoon of Swerve. Mix well and set aside or refrigerate.

5. After 20 minutes take the batter out of the refrigerator. Heat up your waffle iron and if it needs to be greased go ahead and do that.

6. Take 1/4 cup of the mixture and add to the center of the heated waffle iron. Make sure to keep the waffles small so they will be easier to get out of the waffle maker.

7. When it's cooked transfer to a plate and let cool before add whipped cream and strawberries.

Keto Taco Chaffle Recipe

Servings:1

Cooking Time: 8 Minutes

Ingredients:

- 1 egg white
- 1/4 cup Monterey jack cheese, shredded (packed tightly)
- 1/4 cup sharp cheddar cheese, shredded (packed tightly)
- 3/4 tsp water
- 1 tsp coconut flour
- 1/4 tsp baking powder
- 1/8 tsp chili powder
- pinch of salt

Directions:

1. Plug the Dash Mini Waffle Maker in the wall and grease lightly once it is hot.

2. Combine all of the ingredients in a bowl and stir to combine.

3. Spoon out 1/2 of the batter on the waffle maker and close lid. Set a timer for 4 minutes and do not lift the lid until the cooking time is complete. If you do, it will look like the taco chaffle shell isn't setting up properly, but it will. You have to let it cook the entire 4 minutes before lifting the lid.

4. Remove the taco chaffle shell from the waffle iron and set aside. Repeat the same steps above with the rest of the chaffle batter.

5. Turn over a muffin pan and set the taco chaffle shells between the cups to form a taco shell. Allow to set for a few minutes.

6. Remove and serve with the Very Best Taco Meat

7. Enjoy this delicious keto crispy taco chaffle shell with your favorite toppings.

Quick & Easy Keto Sausage Gravy Recipe

Servings:2

Cooking Time: 10 Minutes

Ingredients:

- 1/4 cup breakfast sausage, browned
- 3 tbsp chicken broth
- 2 tbsp heavy whipping cream
- 2 tsp cream cheese, softened
- a dash of garlic powder
- pepper to taste
- a dash of onion powder (optional)

Directions:

1. First, brown some breakfast sausage and set aside 1/4 cup for this recipe. You can use the rest to make sausage patties for later.

2. Add the browned sausage, chicken broth, heavy whipping cream, cream cheese, garlic powder, pepper, and onion powder (optional), in the same skillet and stir continuously until it boils. Then, reduce the heat to medium and let it cook down with the lid off for about 5-7 minutes. If you like

your gravy super thick, add a bit of Xanthan Gum, but be patient, as the gravy will thicken naturally over time.

3. Add salt and pepper to taste and spoon the keto sausage gravy over your favorite low-carb bread.

Keto Chocolate Chip Chaffle Keto Recipe

Servings:1

Cooking Time: 8 Minutes

Ingredients:

- 1 egg
- 1 tbsp heavy whipping cream
- 1/2 tsp coconut flour
- 1 3/4 tsp Lakanto monkfruit golden can use more or less to adjust sweetness
- 1/4 tsp baking powder
- pinch of salt
- 1 tbsp Lily's Chocolate Chips

Directions:

1. Turn on the waffle maker so that it heats up.
2. In a small bowl, combine all ingredients except the chocolate chips and stir well until combined.
3. Grease waffle maker, then pour half of the batter onto the bottom plate of the waffle maker. Sprinkle a few chocolate chips on top and then close.
4. Cook for 3-4 minutes or until the chocolate chip chaffle dessert is golden brown then remove from

waffle maker with a fork, being careful not to burn your fingers.

5. Repeat with the rest of the batter.
6. Let chaffle sit for a few minutes so that it begins to crisp. If desired serve with sugar-free whipped topping.

Keto Chaffle Glazed Donut

Servings:3

Cooking Time: 5 Minutes

Ingredients:

- For the chaffles
- ½ cup Mozzarella cheese shredded
- 1 ounce Cream Cheese
- 2 tablespoon Unflavored whey protein isolate
- 2 tablespoon Swerve confectioners sugar substitute
- ½ teaspoon Baking powder
- ½ teaspoon Vanilla extract
- 1 Egg
- For the glaze topping:
- 2 tablespoon Heavy whipping cream
- 3-4 tablespoon Swerve confectioners sugar substitute
- ½ teaspoon Vanilla extract

Directions:

1. Preheat your mini waffle maker.
2. In a microwave safe bowl, combine the mozzarella cheese and cream cheese. Heat at 30 second

intervals until the cheeses are melted and completely combined.

3. Add the whey protein, 2 tbsp Swerve confectioners sweetener, baking powder to the cheese mixture, and knead with your hands until well incorporated.

4. Place the dough into a mixing bowl, and beat the egg and vanilla into it until a smooth batter forms.

5. Put a third of the batter into the mini waffle maker, and cook for 3-5 minutes until your desired level of doneness has been reached.

6. Repeat step 5 with the remaining ⅔ of the batter, for a total of 3 chaffles made.

7. Beat together the ingredients for the glaze topping, and pour over the chaffles before serving.

Keto Chaffle Churro Recipe

Servings:2

Ingredients:

- 1 egg
- 1/2 cup mozzarella cheese shredded
- 2 tablespoons Swerve Brown Sweetener
- 1/2 teaspoon cinnamon

Directions:

1. Preheat the mini waffle iron.

2. In a small bowl, whip the egg with a fork.

3. Add the shredded cheese to the egg mixture.

4. Place half of the egg mixture in the mini waffle maker and cook it until it's golden brown (about 4 minutes)

5. While the mini Chaffle is cooking, add the Swerve Brown Sweetener and cinnamon in a separate small bowl.

6. Once the Chaffle is done, cut it into slices

7. Serve warm and enjoy!

Keto Chaffle Garlic Cheesy Bread Sticks

Servings:8

Cooking Time: 7 Minutes

Ingredients:

- 1 medium egg
- ½ cup mozzarella cheese grated
- 2 tablespoons almond flour
- ½ teaspoon garlic powder
- ½ teaspoon oregano
- ½ teaspoon salt
- TOPPING
- 2 tablespoons butter, unsalted softened
- ½ teaspoon garlic powder
- ¼ cup mozzarella cheese grated

Directions:

1. Turn on your waffle maker and lightly grease it (I give it a light spray with olive oil)

2. In a bowl, beat the egg.

3. Add the mozzarella, almond flour, garlic powder, oregano and salt and mix well.

4. Spoon the batter into your waffle maker (mine is a square double waffle and this mixture covers both

waffle sections. If you are using a smaller waffle maker spoon half the mixture in at a time).

5. I spoon my mixture into the centre of my waffle maker and gently spread it out towards the edges.

6. Close the lid and cook for 5 minutes.

7. Using tongs, remove the cooked waffles and cut into 4 strips for each waffle.

8. Place the sticks on a tray and pre-heat the grill.

9. Mix the butter with the garlic powder and spread over the sticks.

10. Sprinkle the mozzarella over the sticks and place under the grill for 2-3 minutes until the cheese has melted and bubbling.

11. Eat immediately! (Although we have eaten this heated up but are much nicer freshly made)

Keto Pumpkin Chaffles

Servings:1

Cooking Time: 5 Minutes

Ingredients:

- ½ cup shredded mozzarella cheese
- 1 whole egg beaten
- 1 ½ tablespoons pumpkin purée
- ½ teaspoon Swerve confectioners
- ½ teaspoon vanilla extract
- ¼ teaspoon Pumpkin Pie Spice see my recipe

⅛ teaspoon pure maple extract see **notes**

- Optional: Roasted pecans cinnamon, whip cream and Sugar-Free Maple Syrup for topping

Directions:

1. Turn on your Waffle Maker, (mine makes 4" waffles) and start preparing the batter.

2. Add in all the ingredients, except for the mozzarella cheese to a bowl and whisk. Add in the cheese and mix until well combined.

3. Spray your waffle plates with nonstick spray (I used coconut oil) and add in half the batter to the center. Close the lid and cook for 4-6 minutes, depending on how crispy you want your Chaffles.

4. Remove and cook the second Chaffle. Serve with all or any combination of toppings including butter, Sugar-Free Maple Syrup, roasted pecans, a dusting of ground cinnamon and a dollop of whip cream.

Notes

If you don't have pure maple extract, you can just omit it from the recipe and they will taste great!

Keto Oreo Chaffles

Servings:2

Cooking Time: 8 Minutes

Ingredients:

- 1/2 cup Sugar-Free Chocolate Chips
- 1/2 cup Butter
- 3 Eggs
- 1/4 cup Truvia or other sweetener
- 1 teaspoon Vanilla extract
- CREAM CHEESE FROSTING
- 4 ounces Butter room temperature

- 4 ounces Cream Cheese room temperature
- 1/2 cup Powdered Swerve
- 1/4 cup Heavy Whipping Cream
- 1 teaspoon Vanilla extract

Directions:

1. In a microwave safe bowl, melt butter and chocolate for about 1 minute. Remove and stir well. You really want to use the heat within the butter and chocolate to melt the rest of the clumps. If you microwave until it's all melted, you've overcooked the chocolate. So get a spoon and start stirring. Add 10 seconds if needed but stir well before you decide to do that.
2. In a bowl, add eggs, sweetener, and vanilla and blend until light and frothy.
3. Pour the melted butter and chocolate into the bowl in a slow stream and beat again until it is well-incorporated.
4. Pour about 1/4 of the mixture into a Dash Mini Waffle Maker, and cook for 7-8 minutes, or until crispy.
5. While they cook, make the frosting.
6. Place all the frosting ingredients in the bowl of a food processor and process until smooth and fluffy. You may need to add a little more cream to get the right consistency.
7. Pipe or spread the frosting generously in between two chaffles to make your Oreo Chaffle.
8. Should make two full-size Oreo Chaffles, or four mini Oreo Chaffles.
9. Don't overfill the waffle maker! It will make a huge mess and waste batter. Use no more than 1/4 cup of batter in a Dash Mini.
10. Let the waffles cool some before eating and frosting. This will allow them to crisp up.
11. Use room temp cream cheese and butter to make your frosting.

Pumpkin Chaffle Keto Sugar Cookies

Ingredients:

- Keto Sugar Cookie Ingredients:
- 1 T Butter melted
- 1 T Sweetener
- 1 Egg Yolk
- 1/8 tsp Vanilla Extract
- 1/8 tsp Cake Batter Extract
- 3 T Almond Flour
- 1/8 tsp Baking Powder
- Icing Ingredients:
- 1 T Confectioners Sweetener
- 1/4 tsp Vanilla Extract
- 1-2 tsp Water
- Sprinkles Ingredients:
- 1 T Granular Sweetener mixed with 1 drop of food coloring. Mix well.

Directions:

1. Stir all ingredients together. Let rest for 5 min.
2. Stir again.
3. Refrigerate for 15 mins.
4. Put 1/2 of dough in pumpkin waffle maker.
5. Cook 4 minutes.
6. Repeat. Let cool.
7. Add icing and sprinkles, if desired.

Keto Wookie Cookie Recipe

Servings:12

Ingredients:

- 1 large egg
- 1 tbs sour cream
- 1/2 tsp vanilla
- 2 tbs Oat Fiber not oat flour
- 1/2 tsp coconut flour
- 1/4 tsp baking powder
- 1/4 tsp xanthan gum
- pinch pink salt
- 1 packet splenda sweetener
- 5 drops liquid stevia

Directions:

1. In a small bowl, combine the wet ingredients and whip until fully combined and fluffy.
2. Add the dry ingredients to the wet ingredients and mix until fully combined and smooth.
3. Allow the batter to set for about 5 minutes while you heat up the mini waffle maker. This allows the coconut flour to absorb the liquids properly.

4. Use a small scoop (melon or cookie scoop) to place 3 small scoops on the mini waffle maker.
5. Cook them for a minimum of 3 minutes or until golden brown.
6. You can spread the cookies with sugar free jelly or sprinkle with powdered Sweve keto sweetener too!
7. Or you can frost them with this Keto cream cheese frosting recipe too!

NOTES

Crunchy on the outside and soft on the inside!

The Best Keto Tuna Melt Chaffle Recipe

Servings:2

Ingredients:

- 1 packet Tuna 2.6 oz with no water I used the Jalapeno Tuna for added flavor
- 1/2 cup mozzarella cheese
- 1 egg
- pinch salt

Directions:

1. Preheat the mini waffle maker
2. In a small bowl, add the egg and whip it up.
3. Add the tuna, cheese, and salt and mix well.
4. Optional step for an extra crispy crust: Add a teaspoon of cheese to the mini waffle maker for about 30 seconds before adding the recipe mixture. This will allow the cheese to get crispy when the tuna chaffle is done cooking. I prefer this method!

5. Add 1/2 the mixture to the waffle maker and cook it for a minimum of 4 minutes.

6. Remove it and cook the last tuna chaffle for another 4 minutes.

NOTES

This recipe makes two tuna chaffles. Double the recipe if you are using a full-size waffle maker.

How To Make A Keto Taco Salad Bowl

Servings:2

Ingredients:

- 1/2 cup shredded cheese We used a Colby blend
- 1 egg
- 1/4 tsp onion powder
- 1/8 tsp garlic powder
- Optional: 1 tbs almond flour

Directions:

1. Preheat the waffle bowl maker. There is no need to spray it with non stick cooking spray as long as the bowl isn't scratched.

2. In a small bowl, combine the shredded cheese, egg, seasonings and almond flour, if using. Mix well until fully combined.

3. Note: The almond flour adds more structure to the taco salad shell. If you want a lighter and crispier shell, don't use the almond flour. I personally like them both ways!

4. Place all of the batter into the waffle maker and press the lid closed. DO NOT open the lid for 4 minutes. If you open the lid before the time is up, you will have a gooey mess because the cheese needs time to firm up and create a nice crust.

5. Using a tongs or fork, remove the taco shell from the waffle bowl maker.

6. Unplug the waffle bowl maker when you are done using it.

7. Set the bowl aside to cool and assembly the ingredients you need to fill your taco salad bowl.

NOTES

Keto Taco Salad Bowl Fillings and Toppings

We used leftover taco meat that has been seasoned with our homemade keto taco seasoning, shredded Romaine lettuce, diced tomatoes, sour cream, more shredded cheese and a squirt of our favorite spicy mayo.

Nut-free Keto Cinnamon Roll Chaffles

Servings:3

Cooking Time: 15 Minutes

Ingredients:

- Batter:
- ½ cup (56g) shredded mozzarella cheese
- 2 tbsp (24g) golden monk fruit sweetener
- 2 tbsp (32g) No-Sugar-Added SunButter
- 1 egg

- 1 tbsp (7g) coconut flour
- 2 tsp cinnamon
- ¼ tsp vanilla extract
- ⅛ tsp baking powder
- Frosting:
- ¼ cup (48g) powdered monk fruit sweetener
- 1 tbsp (0.5 oz) cream cheese
- ¾ tbsp (~11g) butter, melted
- ¼ tsp vanilla extract or ⅛ tsp maple extract
- 1 tbsp (15 mL) unsweetened coconut milk (from a container)
- Coating:
- 1 tsp cinnamon
- 1 tsp (4g) golden monk fruit sweetener

Directions:

1. Turn on waffle iron and allow to preheat while preparing batter and frosting.

2. Batter: In a large mixing bowl, mix together all batter ingredients. Set bowl aside to allow batter to set for 3-5 minutes.

3. Frosting: In a separate small mixing bowl, whisk together powdered monk fruit sweetener, cream cheese, butter, and vanilla or maple extract until smooth. Pour in coconut milk and whisk all ingredients again until well-combined. Set aside.

4. Final Steps: Generously coat preheated waffle iron with nonstick cooking spray. Divide chaffle batter into 3 servings and spoon 1 part into waffle iron, leaving a small gap at the edge as batter will expand while cooking. Cook batter until chaffle is golden brown, about 2-4 minutes.

5. Open waffle iron lid and allow chaffle to cool in waffle iron for about 30 seconds before carefully removing chaffle at the edges with a fork and transferring to a plate. While warm, sprinkle chaffles with cinnamon and monk fruit sweetener coating. Once slightly cooled, drizzle icing atop chaffles.

Recipe Notes:

SunButter Substitution: If you don't have a nut allergy, you can substitute in unsweetened almond butter or unsweetened peanut butter for SunButter at a 1:1 ratio.

Net Carbs: One chaffle contains 3.4 grams of net carbs.

Refrigerator Storage: Store these keto chaffles in the refrgierator in an airtight container or freezer bag and eat within 3 days.

Freezer Storage: Store these chaffles in a freezer bag or airtight container and use parchment paper to separate each waffle to avoid them sticking together. Store in the freezer for up to 2 months.

Reheating Refrigerated or Frozen Chaffles: To reheat refrigerated chaffles, place in a toaster (only use a toaster if you have not pre-drizzled the chaffles with icing), a preheated toaster oven, or a preheated oven and heat until warmed throughout. I would not suggest reheating in the microwave as they will become very, very chewy. If frozen, unthaw chaffles in the refrigerator before reheating.

Keto Big Mac Recipe With Homemade Keto Big Mac Sauce

Servings:1

Cooking Time: 10 Minutes

Ingredients:

- Keto Big Mac Chaffles Ingredients:
- 2 Keto Burger patties
- 2 tablespoons Keto Big Mac Sauce
- 3 Garlic Cheddar chaffles
- 2 slices American cheese
- 1/4 cup iceberg lettuce
- 4 dill pickles slices
- 1/2 tablespoon onions minced
- sesame seeds optional
- Big Mac Chaffle Ingredients:
- 2 egg
- 1/2 teaspoon garlic powder
- 1 cup shredded cheddar
- Keto Big Mac Sauce Ingredients:
- 1/2 cup mayonnaise
- 1/2 tablespoon mustard
- 1/2 tablespoon relish
- 1 teaspoon vinegar
- 1/4 teaspoon onion powder
- 1/4 teaspoon garlic powder
- 1/4 teaspoon paprika
- Big Mac Burger Ingredients:
- 1/4 pound ground beef
- salt to taste
- pepper to taste

Directions:

1. How to Make Keto Big Mac Recipe
2. How to Make Big Mac Chaffles
3. Heat up your dash mini waffle maker.
4. In a small bowl mix the egg, garlic powder, and shredded cheddar cheese.
5. Once the dash waffle maker is heated up add in half the chaffle mixture. Cook for 4 minutes and remove. Repeat this step with the chaffle mixture two more times.
6. How to Make Big Mac Burger
7. Preheat a pan over medium heat. Divided the beef into two chaffle sized patties, season them with salt and pepper. Cook burgers for about three minutes on each side. Top the burgers with the cheese slices and remove from the heat.
8. How to Make Keto Big Mac Sauce
9. In a small bowl mix the mayonnaise, mustard, relish, vinegar, onion powder, garlic powder and paprika and set aside.
10. How to Assemble Keto Big Mac Burger Chaffle
11. Spread the sauce on the top of two of the chaffles. Top the first chaffle with lettuce, onion, pickles, and burger. Repeat this again with chaffle, lettuce, onion, pickles burger, and the last chaffle.
12. You can top the last chaffle with sesame seeds if you want to.

Keto Lemon Chaffle Recipe

Servings:4

Ingredients:

- Chaffle Cake:
- 2 oz cream cheese room temp and softened
- 2 eggs
- 2 tsp butter melted
- 2 tbs coconut flour
- 1 tsp monkfruit powdered confectioners blend (add more if you like it sweeter)
- 1 tsp baking powder
- 1/2 tsp lemon extract
- 20 drops cake batter extract
- Chaffle Frosting:
- 1/2 cup heavy whipping cream
- 1 tbs monkfruit powdered confectioners blend
- 1/4 tsp lemon extract
- Optional
- Add lemon peel for extra flavor!

Directions:

1. Preheat the mini waffle maker
2. Add all of the ingredients for the chaffle cake in a blender and mix it until the batter is nice and smooth. This should only take a couple of minutes.
3. Use an ice cream scoop and fill the waffle iron with one full scoop of batter. This size of the ice cream scoop is about 3 tablespoons and fits perfectly in the mini waffle maker.
4. While the chaffles are cooking, start making the frosting.
5. In a medium-size bowl, add the chaffle frosting ingredients.
6. Mix the ingredients until the frosting is thick with peaks.
7. All the chaffles to completely cool before frosting the cake.
8. Optional: Add lemon peel for extra flavor!

Keto Vanilla Twinkie Copycat Chaffle Recipe

Servings:6

Ingredients:

- 2 tablespoons butter melted (cooled)
- 2 ounces cream cheese softened
- 2 large eggs room temp
- 1 teaspoon vanilla extract
- 1/2 teaspoon Vanilla Cupcake Extract optional
- 1/4 cup Lakanto Confectioners
- Pinch of pink salt
- 1/4 cup almond flour
- 2 tablespoons coconut flour
- 1 teaspoon baking powder

Directions:

1. Preheat the Corndog Maker.
2. Melt the butter and let it cool a minute.
3. Whisk the eggs into the butter until creamy.

4. Add vanilla, extract, sweetener, salt and then blend well.

5. Add Almond flour, coconut flour, and baking powder.

6. Blend until well incorporated.

7. Add ~2 tbs batter to each well and spread across evenly.

8. Close lid, lock and let cook 4 minutes.

9. Remove and cool on a rack.

Keto Chocolate Chaffle Recipe

Servings:2

Cooking Time: 8 Minutes

Ingredients:

- 1/2 cup Sugar-Free Chocolate Chips
- 1/2 cup Butter
- 3 Eggs
- 1/4 cup Truvia or other sweetener
- 1 teaspoon Vanilla extract

Directions:

1. In a microwave safe bowl, melt butter and chocolate for about 1 minute. Remove and stir well. You really want to use the heat within the butter and chocolate to melt the rest of the clumps. If you microwave until it's all melted, you've overcooked the chocolate. So get a spoon and start stirring. Add 10 seconds if needed but stir well before you decide to do that.

2. In a bowl, add eggs, sweetener, and vanilla and blend until light and frothy.

3. Pour the melted butter and chocolate into the bowl in a slow stream and beat again until it is well-incorporated.

4. Pour about 1/4 of the mixture into a Dash Mini Waffle Maker, and cook for 7-8 minutes, or until crispy.

5. Should make 4 waffles, with a little batter left over.

6. Serve these with whipped cream or syrup when they're warm for best results.

7. Don't over-microwave the chocolate, or it will burn. Only cook and stir until it's just smooth and melted.

8. These freeze well! Make a big batch and save some in the freezer to heat up later.

Keto Rye Bread Chaffle Recipe

Servings:1

Ingredients:

- 1 egg
- 2 tablespoons almond flour
- 1 tablespoon melted butter
- 1 tablespoon mozzarella cheese
- pinch salt
- pinch garlic powder
- 1/2 teaspoon baking powder
- 1/2 teaspoon caraway seeds

Directions:

1. Preheat mini waffle maker.

2. Mix all rye bread chaffle ingredients in a small bowl.

3. Place 1/2 the mixture into a preheated mini waffle maker.

4. Cook for 4 minutes.

5. Serve warm.

Sausage Egg And Cheese Keto Copycat Mcgriddle Recipe

Servings:2

Ingredients:

- Copycat McGriddle Chaffle Ingredients:
- 1 egg
- 1 tablespoon almond flour
- 1 tablespoon coconut flour
- 1 ounce cream cheese
- 2 tablespoons mozzarella
- 1/2 teaspoon sukrin gold brown
- 1/2 teaspoon baking powder
- 1 1/2 tablespoons keto-friendly maple syrup
- Additional Ingredients:
- breakfast sausage patties
- eggs scrambled
- cheddar cheese shredded
- Other Protein Options
- bacon slices
- keto fried chicken strips

Directions:

1. Mix all copycat mcgriddle chaffle ingredients together in a small bowl.

2. Place 1/4 of the mixture into a small waffle iron and cook for 2 1/2 to 3 minutes.

3. Cook breakfast sausage patty until brown.

4. Scramble and cook eggs.

5. Place breakfast sausage patty (cook until brown), egg (scramble and cook) and cheese.

6. Place cooked egg on cooked sausage in your pan and add cheese to the top.

7. Cook covered on low until the cheese melts.

8. Then place between the chaffles.

9. Serve and enjoy!

Keto Parmesan Garlic Chaffles - 3 Ways

Servings:1

Cooking Time: 4 Minutes

Ingredients:

- ½ cup shredded mozzarella cheese
- 1 whole egg beaten
- ¼ cup grated Parmesan cheese
- 1 teaspoon Italian Seasoning
- ¼ teaspoon garlic powder

Directions:

1. Turn on your Waffle Maker, (mine makes 4″ waffles) and start preparing the batter.

2. Add in all the ingredients, except for the mozzarella cheese to a bowl and whisk. Add in the cheese and mix until well combined.

3. Spray your waffle plates with nonstick spray (I used coconut oil) and add in half the batter to the center. Close the lid and cook for 3-5 minutes, depending on how crispy you want your Chaffles.

4. To serve, there are a couple of options. One is to serve with a drizzle of olive oil, grated Parmesan cheese and fresh chopped parsley or basil.

Notes

Variations

Italian Chaffle Sandwich

Prepare the base recipe as noted above. Add your favor cold cuts, lettuce, tomato, whatever you like. I added ham, salami, lettuce and roasted red pepper.

Chaffle Breadsticks

Prepare the base recipe as noted above. Cut each chaffle into 4 sticks and serve with a side of Low Carb Marinara Sauce.

Chaffle Bruschetta

Prepare the base recipe as noted above. Mix together 3-4 cherry tomatoes, chopped, ½ teaspoon fresh basil chopped, splash of olive oil and a pinch of salt. Serve over the top of the chaffles as prepared above.

Keto Chaffle Recipe

Ingredients:

- 1 large egg
- 1/2 c. shredded cheese
- Pinch of salt
- Seasoning to taste

Directions:

1. Preheat the mini waffle maker.

2. In a bowl- whisk the egg until beaten.

3. Shred the cheese (any flavor or combination you like).

4. Add the cheese, salt, and seasoning to the egg, then mix well.

5. Scoop half of the mixture on the waffle maker, spread evenly.

6. Cook 3-4 minutes, until done to your liking (crispy).

7. Pull it off and let cool.

8. Add the rest of batter and cook the 2nd waffle.

9. Enjoy!

Keto Strawberry Shortcake Chaffles

Servings:1

Ingredients:

- 1 egg
- 1/3 cup shredded mozzarella cheese
- 1 tbsp almond flour
- 1 tbsp cream cheese
- 1/2 tbsp Swerve (or any low carb sweetener)
- 1/4 tsp baking powder

- 3-4 sliced strawberries
- Keto Whipped Cream
- 1 cup heavy whipping cream
- 1 tbsp Swerve (or any low carb sweetener)
- 1/2 tsp vanilla extract

Directions:

1. Preheat your mini waffle maker. Mix all of your chaffle ingredients together in a small bowl (egg, mozzarella, almond flour, cream cheese, low carb sweetener and baking powder). Grease your waffle maker with a non-stick spray and pour half of the batter in. Cook until the automatic timer or light goes off; repeat for next waffle.

2. While the chaffles are cooling, whip the heavying whipping cream, low carb sweetener and vanilla extact together with a hand mixer until stiff peaks form (this takes about 5 minutes). *See Notes Below

3. Layer the sweet chaffles, whipped cream and sliced strawberries together. Enjoy!

Recipe Notes

*The recipe for the keto whipped cream makes at least 4 servings, so feel free to cut the recipe down if desired. I prefer to just make a large batch so that I have leftovers for something else later like my morning coffee or my favorite crispy breakfast chaffles.

If you happen to have a cake batter extract or strawberry extract stocked in your pantry, try adding 1/2 a teaspoon to the chaffle batter. Yum!

Keto Cauliflower Chaffles Recipe

Servings:2

Cooking Time: 4 Minutes

Ingredients:

- 1 cup riced cauliflower
- 1/4 teaspoon Garlic Powder
- 1/4 teaspoon Ground Black Pepper
- 1/2 teaspoon Italian Seasoning
- 1/4 teaspoon Kosher Salt
- 1/2 cup shredded mozzarella cheese or shredded mexican blend cheese
- 1 Eggs
- 1/2 cup shredded parmesan cheese

Directions:

1. Add all ingredients into a blender.

2. Sprinkle 1/8 cup parmesan cheese into the waffle maker. Make sure to cover the bottom of the waffle iron as shown in the video.

3. Fill the waffle maker with the cauliflower mixture.

4. Add another sprinkle of parmesan cheese on top of the mixture.

5. Cook for 4-5 minutes, or until crispy.

6. Makes 4 mini chaffles, or two regular full-size chaffles.

7. These work great in a mini waffle maker (I use the Mini Dash Waffle Maker), but you can also use a regular size one as well.

8. These freeze well. Make a big batch and freeze them for later.

9. TIPS AND TRICKS FOR HOW TO MAKE THE BEST CAULIFLOWER CHAFFLES EVER

10. Patience. That's the best tip. They don't take very long but if you want a crisp keto waffle, you are just going to have to be a little patient and let it take the 5-7 minutes that it takes to crisp up. Just when you think it's done? Give it another minute or two. Don't rush.

11. Layering. Don't skimp on the cheese on the top and bottom. Use more than the recipe calls for if you think you need it. It's the crispy cheese on the bottom and top that will make them crispy.

12. Shallow waffles. If you want crispy waffles, the shallower the waffle iron, the easier/faster it is to crisp up the chaffle.

13. No overfilling. Overfilled chaffle makersâ€¦well, they overflow of course. Which makes a huge mess! So if in doubt, underfill rather than overfill. No more than 1/4 cup of TOTAL ingredients at a time.

14. No peeking. I can tell you from LOTS of personal experience, that opening the waffle iron every 30 seconds â€œjust to checkâ€ doesn't hep the chaffle cook any faster. Your best bet is to not even open it for 4-5 minutes.

15. No steaming. if you're using the Dash mini, the little blue light goes out when it's mostly cooked, but most importantly, the chaffle stops steaming quite so much. That's a good sign that it's done.

16. Get hot. Wait until the waffle iron is hot before you add ingredients, and they're a lot less likely to stick, and a lot easier to clean up.

17. Mat it. Okay so about that overflow. I do find that it happens to me more often than I would like! One thing that has made cleanup easier for me has been to put a silicone trivet underneath.

18. Crispy Cooling. Allow the chaffles to cool before eating. They get crisper as they cool, so try not to stuff the hot chaffle into your mouth right away.

19. Make lots. Make enough to share, everyone will want them, no matter whether they're keto or not.

Keto Cornbread Chaffle Recipe

Servings:2

Ingredients:

- 1 egg

- 1/2 cup cheddar cheese shredded (or mozzarella)

- 5 slices jalapeno optional - picked or fresh

- 1 tsp Frank's Red hot sauce

- 1/4 tsp corn extract this is the secret ingredient that is a must!

- pinch salt

Directions:

1. Preheat the mini waffle maker

2. In a small bowl, whip the egg.

3. Add the remaining ingredients and mix it until it's well incorporated.

4. Add a teaspoon of shredded cheese to the waffle maker for 30 seconds before adding the mixture. This will create a nice and crisp crust that is absolutely fantastic!

5. Add half the mixture to the preheated waffle maker.

6. Cook it for a minimum of 3 to 4 minutes. The longer you cook it the more crispy it gets.

NOTES

Serve warm and enjoy!

Keto Pizza Chaffle Recipe

Servings:2

Ingredients:

- 1 egg
- 1/2 cup mozzarella cheese shredded
- Just a pinch of Italian seasoning
- No sugar added pizza sauce about 1 tablespoon
- Top with more shredded cheese pepperoni (or any of your favorite toppings)

Directions:

1. Preheat the Dash waffle maker.

2. In a small bowl, whip the egg and seasonings together.

3. Mix in the shredded cheese.

4. Add a tsp of shredded cheese to the preheated waffle maker and let it cook for about 30 seconds. This will help to create a more crisp crust.

5. Add half the mixture to the waffle maker and cook it for about 4 minutes until it's golden brown and slightly crispy!

6. Remove the waffle and add the remaining mixture to the waffle maker to make the second chaffle.

7. Top with a tablespoon of pizza sauce, shredded cheese, and pepperoni. Microwave it on high for about 20 seconds and voila! Instant Chaffle PIZZA!

New & Improved Keto Waffles

Servings:2

Ingredients:

- 1 egg
- 1/4 cup shredded mozzarella cheese
- 1 tbsp sugar-free vanilla pudding mix (dry)
- 1/4 tsp cake batter flavor

Directions:

1. Preheat your mini waffle maker and mix everything together in a small bowl.

2. Grease the waffle maker with a non-stick spray and pour half of the batter in. Cook until the automatic timer or light goes off; repeat for next chaffle.

3. Serve with sugar free syrup. Enjoy!

Recipe Notes

I had a hard time finding flavored extracts at the grocery store, but discovered that Walmart has a huge selection including the cake batter flavor.

Easy Keto Peanut Butter Chaffles

Servings:2

Ingredients:

- 1 egg
- 2 tbsp peanut butter or nut butter (without added sugar)
- 1/3 cup shredded mozzarella cheese
- 1 tbsp monk fruit (or low carb sweetener of your choice)
- 1/2 tsp vanilla extract

Directions:

1. Preheat your mini waffle maker and mix everything together in a small bowl.
2. Use a non-stick spray to grease the waffle maker and then pour HALF of the batter in. Allow it to cook for 3-4 minutes or until the automatic timer or lights goes off; repeat for next waffle.
3. Serve alone or with a little butter and sugar free syrup!

The Best 3 Ingredient Keto Waffles

Servings:2

Ingredients:

- 1 large egg
- 1/2 cup freshly shredded cheese (I like mozzarella)
- 1 heaping tbsp of almond flour

Directions:

1. Preheat your waffle maker (a mini waffle maker is best and should make 2 small waffles).
2. Crack your egg into a bowl and whisk until well beaten. Add the almond flour and mix again. Next, stir in the cheese until well combined.
3. Spray your waffle maker with non-stick spray and sprinkle a little cheese directly onto the griddle. Pour half of the mixture in and sprinkle with more cheese; close the lid and cook for 2-3 minutes or until your automatic timer goes off. Repeat for next waffle.
4. Enjoy with a little butter and sugar-free syrup.

Recipe Notes

These can also be used to replace bread in a sandwich. Shredded mozzarella or cheddar works well for this recipe. If you're eating them as a traditional waffle I'd recommend mozzarella. To make them a little more savory, try using cheddar.

Want to switch out the almond flour for coconut flour? Use teaspoons instead of tablespoons. Basically, cut the amount used to 1/3.

Here are a few additions you may consider to flavor your waffles: vanilla extract, cinnamon, pumpkin spice, cocoa powder, sugar-free chocolate chips, berries or a low carb sweetener.

These are freezable, and can be reheated in your toaster or on a hot skillet.

Easy Keto Pizza Chaffles

Servings:2

Ingredients:

- 1 egg
- 1 heaping tbsp almond flour
- 1/2 cup shredded mozzarella (plus more for topping)
- 1 tbsp grated parmesan
- 1/8 tsp Italian seasoning
- 1/8 tsp garlic powder
- pizza toppings of your choice

Directions:

1. Preheat your oven to 400 degrees and turn on your mini waffle maker.
2. In a small bowl, whisk the egg together and then combine with the rest of the ingredients.
3. Once your mini waffle maker is hot, spinkle the griddle with a little shedded mozzarella.
4. Pour HALF of the batter in and then sprinkle with more cheese. Close the lid and cook until the automatic timer or light goes off; repeat for next waffle.
5. Place the chaffles on a baking sheet and allow them to cool for a few minutes (so that they don't get soggy), and then spread with a low carb pizza sauce, shredded cheese and the toppings of your choice.
6. Bake for 3-4 minutes and then an additional minute or two with the broiler on to brown the cheese.
7. Sprinkle with a little more Italian seasonig and enjoy!

Keto Pumpkin Chaffle Cake

Servings:4

Cooking Time: 12 Minutes

Ingredients:

- FOR THE CAKE:
- 2 large eggs
- ¼ cup pumpkin puree
- 2 tablespoons brown sugar substitute
- 2 teaspoons pumpkin pie spice
- 2 teaspoons coconut flour
- ½ teaspoon vanilla
- 1 cup finely shredded mozzarella cheese
- FOR THE FROSTING:
- 4 ounces cream cheese, room temperature
- ¼ cup butter, room temperature
- ½ cup powdered sweetener
- 1 teaspoon vanilla
- ¼ cup chopped pecans

Directions:

1. Plug in waffle maker to preheat. Spray with non-stick spray.
2. Add the eggs, pumpkin puree, sweetener, pumpkin pie spice, coconut flour, and vanilla to a small bowl and whisk well to combine.
3. Stir in the cheese.

4. Spoon 1/4 of the batter into the hot waffle iron and smooth the batter out to the edges of the waffle iron.

5. Close the iron and cook for 3 minutes.

6. Remove the waffle and set aside. Repeat with remaining batter.

7. Allow chaffles to cool before frosting.

8. To make the frosting, beat together the cream cheese and butter with an electric mixer until smooth and creamy. Beat in the powdered sweetener and vanilla until well combined.

9. Spread the frosting over the top of one chaffle and top with another chaffle. Repeat the layers ending with a layer of frosting.

10. Sprinkle with chopped pecans to decorate.

Notes

We prefer to use finely shredded cheese in chaffles as we find it gives the final product a better texture.

Keto Chaffle Blt Sandwich

Servings:1

Cooking Time: 10 Minutes

Ingredients:

- For the chaffles
- 1 egg
- 1/2 cup Cheddar cheese, shredded
- For the sandwich
- 2 strips bacon
- 1-2 slices tomato
- 2-3 pieces lettuce
- 1 tablespoon mayonnaise

Directions:

1. Preheat the waffle maker according to manufacturer instructions..

2. In a small mixing bowl, mix together egg and shredded cheese. Stir until well combined.

3. Pour one half of the waffle batter into the waffle maker. Cook for 3-4 minutes or until golden brown. Repeat with the second half of the batter.

4. In a large pan over medium heat, cook the bacon until crispy, turning as needed. Remove to drain on paper towels.

5. Assemble the sandwich with lettuce, tomato, and mayonnaise. Enjoy!

NOTES

If you are using a larger size waffle maker, you may be able to cook the whole amount of batter in one waffle. This will vary with the size of your machine.

CHAFFLE CAKE RECIPES

Tiramisu Chaffle Cake Recipe

Servings:4

Ingredients:

- 2 tbs Unsalted Butter melted
- 2 tsp Instant Coffee Dry Mix
- 1 oz Cream Cheese softened
- 2 Large Eggs room temp
- 1 tsp Pure Vanilla Extract
- 1/2 tsp Hazelnut Extract optional
- 1/4 c. Blanched Almond Flour fine
- 2 tbs Coconut Flour
- 1 tbs Organic Cacao Powder
- 2 tbs Powdered Monkfruit Sweetener by Lakanto
- 1 tsp Baking Powder
- 1/8 tsp Himalayan Fine Pink Salt
- 4 oz. Mascarpone Cheese by Cello
- 1/4 c. Lakanto Powdered Sweetener
- 1/2 tsp Pure Vanilla Extract
- 1/2 tbs Organic Cacao Powder
- 1/2 tsp Instant Coffee Dry Mix

Directions:

1. Melt the butter in a microwave safe dish, then stir in instant coffee.
2. In a medium mixing bowl- add cream cheese, eggs and extracts. Blend well.
3. Add all dry ingredients and mix until incorporated.
4. Scoop 2 heaping tbs of batter into waffle maker, cook 3-4 mins each.
5. Make the chaffles and let cool while making the frosting.
6. In a separate bowl- add Mascarpone, sweetener, vanilla.
7. Split cream into 2 separate bowls if you want two layers of frosting.
8. Add cacao and instant coffee into second bowl, blend well.
9. Layer the white cream over each chaffle and stack.
10. (optionallRefrigerate the cake for 20 minutes.
11. Spread the second cream over top and around the sides.
12. Put cake in the fridge for 20-30 minutes to let the frosting set up.
13. Cut into slices and enjoy!

Keto Strawberry Cake Chaffle Recipe

Servings:2

Ingredients:

- Chaffle Ingredients:
- 1 egg
- 1 ounce cream cheese
- 1/2 tsp vanilla
- 1 tbs almond flour
- 1 tbs monk fruit confectioners blend

- 10 drops OOOFlavors Strawberry Souffle
- 10 drops OOOFlavors Cake Batter
- 2 drops red food coloring optional
- Top with sliced strawberries optional
- Strawberry Frosting Ingredients:
- 1 tbs cream cheese room temp
- 1 tbs butter room temp
- 1 tbs monk fruit confectioners blend
- 9 drops OOOFlavors Strawberry Souffle

Directions:

1. In a small bowl, add the egg and use a hand whisk to mix it until fluffy.
2. Add the remaining ingredients and mix well until it's all fully combined.
3. Preheat the mini waffle maker.
4. Pour half the mixture into the mini waffle maker (or pour all of the mixture into a large waffle maker) and cook it for about 3 minutes until it's done.
5. Repeat that step to cook the other strawberry cake chaffle.
6. Allow both chaffle cakes to cool before frosting them.
7. Double the recipe to make a tall cake!
8. Make the strawberry frosting while the chaffles are cooling.
9. In a small bowl combine all the ingredients and mix it with a small hand mixture. This recipe can be doubled or tripled if you prefer more frosting.
10. Frost the cooled cake and top with strawberries!

11. Enjoy!

Keto Chocolate Waffle Cake Recipe

Servings:4

Ingredients:

- 2 Tbs Cocoa
- 2 Tbs Monkfruit Confectioner's
- 1 egg
- 1/4 Tsp Baking Powder
- 1 Tbs heavy whipping cream
- Add Keto Ice Cream of choice

Directions:

1. In a small bowl, whip up the egg.
2. Add the remaining ingredients and mix well until the batter is smooth and creamy.
3. Pour half the batter in a mini waffle maker and cook it for 2 1/2 to 3 minutes until it's fully cooked.
4. Allow the chaffle waffles to fully cool before placing ice cream in the center.
5. Freeze until solid.
6. Serve cold and enjoy!

Keto Red Velvet Waffle Cake Recipe

Servings:2

Ingredients:

- 2 Tbs Dutch Processed Cocoa
- 2 Tbs Monkfruit Confectioner's
- 1 egg
- 2 drops super red food coloring optional
- 1/4 Tsp Baking Powder
- 1 Tbs heavy whipping cream
- Frosting Ingredients:
- 2 Tbs Monkfruit Confectioners
- 2 Tbs Cream Cheese softened and room temp
- 1/4 tsp clear vanilla

Directions:

1. In a small bowl, whip up the egg.
2. Add the remaining ingredients and mix well until the batter is smooth and creamy.
3. Pour half the batter in a mini waffle maker and cook it for 2 1/2 to 3 minutes until it's fully cooked.
4. In a separate small bowl, add the sweetener, cream cheese, and vanilla. Mix the frosting until everything is well incorporated.
5. Spread the frosting on the waffle cake after it has completely cooled down to room temperature.

Strawberry Shortcake Chaffle Recipe

Servings:2

Ingredients:

- 1 egg
- 1/4 cup mozzarella cheese
- 1 tbs cream cheese
- 1/4 tsp baking powder
- 2 strawberries sliced
- 1 tsp strawberry extract

Directions:

1. Preheat waffle maker.
2. In a small bowl, whip the egg.
3. Add the remaining ingredients.
4. Spray the waffle maker with non stick cooking spray.
5. Divide mixture in half.
6. Cook half the mixture for about 4 minutes or until golden brown.

NOTES

Optional Glaze: 1 tbs cream cheese warmed in the microwave for 15 seconds, 1/4 tsp strawberry extract, and 1 tbs monkfruit confectioners blend.

Mix and spread over the warm waffle.

Optional Cream Cheese Frosting: 1 tbs cream cheese (room temp), 1/4 tsp strawberry extract, 1 tbs room temp butter (room temp), and 1 tbs monkfruit confectioners blend. Mix all ingredients together and spread on top of the waffle.

You can also top it with simple whipped cream and strawberries.

Homemade whipped cream: 1 cup heavy whipping cream, 1 tsp vanilla, 1 tbs monkfruit confectioners blend. Whip until it forms peaks. Easy peasy!

Banana Pudding Chaffle Cake

Ingredients:

- Pudding Ingredients:
- 1 large egg yolk
- 1/2 cup heavy whipping cream
- 3 T powdered sweetener
- 1/4 - 1/2 tsp xanthan gum
- 1/2 tsp banana extract
- Banana Chaffle Ingredients:
- 1 oz cream cheese softened
- 1/4 cup mozzarella cheese shredded
- 1 egg beaten
- 1 tsp banana extract
- 2 T sweetener
- 1 tsp baking powder
- 4 T almond flour

Directions:

1. Combine the heavy cream, powdered sweetener and egg yolk in a small saucepan. Whisk constantly until the sweetener dissolves and mixture thickens.
2. Simmer 1 minute. Add the xanthan gum and whisk.
3. Remove from heat and add a pinch of salt and the banana extract and stir well.

4. Transfer to a glass dish and cover surface of the pudding with plastic wrap. Refrigerate.
5. Mix all ingredients together. Cook in preheated mini waffle maker.

Coconut Cream Cake Chaffle Recipe

Servings:6

Ingredients:

- Chaffles:
- 2 eggs
- 1 ounce cream cheese softened to room temperature
- 2 tablespoons finely shredded unsweetened coconut
- 2 tablespoons powdered sweetener blend
- 1 tablespoon melted butter or coconut oil
- 1/2 teaspoon coconut extract
- 1/2 teaspoon vanilla extract
- Filling:
- 1/3 cup coconut milk
- 1/3 cup unsweetened almond or cashew milk
- 2 eggs yolks
- 2 tablespoons powdered sweetener blend
- 1/4 teaspoon xanthan gum
- 2 teaspoons butter
- Pinch of salt
- 1/4 cup finely shredded unsweetened coconut
- Optional garnishes:
- Sugar-free whipped cream

- 1 tablespoon finely shredded unsweetened coconut toasted until lightly brown

Directions:

1. For the chaffles:
2. Heat mini Dash waffle iron until thoroughly hot.
3. Beat all chaffle ingredients together in a small bowl.
4. Add a heaping 2 tablespoons batter to waffle iron and cook until golden brown and the waffle iron stops steaming, about 5 minutes.
5. Repeat 3 times to make 4 chaffles. You only need 3 for the recipe.
6. For the filling:
7. Heat the coconut and almond milk in a small saucepan over medium-low heat. It should be steaming hot, but not simmering or boiling.
8. In a separate bowl, beat the egg yolks together lightly. While whisking the milk constantly, slowly drizzle the egg yolks into the milk.
9. Heat, stirring constantly until the mixture thickens slightly. Do not boil. Whisk in the sweetener.
10. While whisking constantly, slowly sprinkle in the xanthan gum. Continue to cook for 1 minute.
11. Remove from the heat and add the remaining ingredients.
12. Pour coconut cream filling into a container, cover the surface with plastic wrap and refrigerate until cool. The plastic wrap prevents a skin from forming on the filling. The mixture will thicken as is cools.
13. Cake assembly:
14. Spread 1/3 of the filling over each of 3 chaffles, stack them together to make a cake, top with whipped cream and garnish with toasted coconut.

Keto Boston Cream Pie Chaffle Cake Recipe

Ingredients:

- Chaffle Cake Ingredients:
- 2 eggs
- 1/4 cup almond flour
- 1 tsp coconut flour
- 2 tbsp melted butter
- 2 tbsp cream cheese room temp
- 20 drops Boston Cream extract
- 1/2 tsp vanilla extract
- 1/2 tsp baking powder
- 2 tbsp swerve confectioners sweetener or monkfruit
- 1/4 tsp Xanthan powder
- Custard Ingredients:
- 1/2 cup heavy whipping cream
- 1/2 tsp Vanilla extract
- 1 /2 tbs Swerve confectioners Sweetener
- 2 Egg Yolks
- 1/8 tsp Xanthan Gum
- Ganache Ingredients:
- 2 tbs heavy whipping cream
- 2 tbs Unsweetened Baking chocolate bar chopped
- 1 tbs Swerve Confectioners Sweetener

Directions:

1. Preheat the mini waffle iron to make cake chaffles first.

2. In a blender, combine all the cake ingredients and blend it on high until it's smooth and creamy. This should only take a couple of minutes.

3. On the stovetop, heat the heavy whipping cream to a boil. While it's heating, whisk the egg yolks and Swerve together in a separate small bowl.

4. Once the cream is boiling, pour half of it into the egg yolks. Make sure you are whisking it together while you pour in the mixture slowly.

5. Pour the egg and cream mixture back into the stovetop pan into the rest of the cream and stir continuously for another 2-3 minutes.

6. Take the custard off the heat and whisk in your vanilla & xanthan gum. Then set it aside to cool and thicken.

7. Put ingredients for the ganache in a small bowl. Microwave for 20 seconds, stir. Repeat if needed. Careful not to overheat the ganache and burn it. Only do 20 seconds at a time until it's fully melted.

8. Assemble your Boston Cream Pie Chaffle Cake and Enjoy!!

Chocolate Chip Cookie Chaffle Cake Recipe

Ingredients:

- 1 T Butter melted
- 1 T Golden Monkfruit sweetener
- 1 Egg Yolk
- 1/8 tsp Vanilla Extract
- 1/8 tsp Cake Batter Extract
- 3 T Almond Flour
- 1/8 tsp Baking Powder
- 1 T Chocolate Chips sugar free
- Whipped Cream Frosting Ingredients:
- 1 tsp unflavored gelatin
- 4 tsp Cold Water
- 1 Cup HWC
- 2 T Confectioners Sweetener

Directions:

1. Chocolate Chip Cookie Chaffle Cake

2. Cake Directions:

3. Mix everything together and cook in a mini waffle iron for 4 mins. Repeat for each layer. I chose to make

4. Whipped Cream Frosting Directions:

5. Place your beaters and your mixing bowl in the freezer for about 15 minutes to allow them to cool.

6. In a microwave-safe bowl, sprinkle the gelatin over the cold water. Stir, and allow to "bloom". This takes about 5 minutes.

7. Microwave the gelatin mixture for 10 seconds. It will become a liquid. Stir to make sure everything is dissolved.

8. In your chilled mixing bowl, begin whipping the cream on a low speed. Add in the confectioner's sugar.

9. Move to a higher speed and watch for good peaks to begin to form.

10. Once the whipping cream is starting to peak, switch back to a lower speed and slowly drizzle the melted liquid gelatin mixture in. Once it's in, switch back to a higher speed and continue to beat until it's reached stiff peaks.

11. Place in piping bags and pipe on your cake.

NOTES

I only used 1/2 of the whipped cream for this recipe.

Strawberry Shortcake Chaffles

Servings:1

Cooking Time: 6 Minutes

Ingredients:

- 1 tbsp Coconut Flour
- 1 tbsp Sweetener sugar alternative or preferred sweetener
- 1/4 tsp Baking Powder
- 1 tbsp Strawberry Powder
- 1 Egg room temp
- 1 oz Cream Cheese room temp
- 1/2 tsp Vanilla Extract
- 1 Strawberry
- 2 tbsp Whip Cream

Directions:

1. Gather all the ingredients. Note – For quick room temperature eggs, submerge egg in warm water for 3-5 min. For quick room temperature cream cheese, take the amount needed and microwave for 10-15 sec.

2. Prepare Strawberry Powder if needed.

3. Slice strawberries into slices and set them aside.

4. Plug-in Dash Mini Waffle Maker to pre-heat.

5. In a small mixing bowl, add Coconut Flour, sweetener, Baking Powder, Strawberry Powder and mix.

6. Next, add egg, cream cheese, Vanilla Extract and mix with a whisk until well combined.

7. Pour batter into waffle iron and cook for 2.5 - 3 minutes until browned to liking. Repeat until all the batter is used.

8. Once the chaffles are done, apply whipping cream to one of the chaffles, followed by slices of the strawberries and finishing by sandwiching the other chaffle on top. Enjoy with your favorite sugar-free syrup or just as is!

Keto Birthday Cake Chaffle Recipe

Servings:4

Ingredients:

- Chaffle Cake Ingredients:
- makes mini four cakes
- 2 eggs
- 1/4 cup almond flour
- 1 tsp coconut flour
- 2 tbsp melted butter
- 2 tbsp cream cheese room temp
- 1 tsp cake batter extract
- 1/2 tsp vanilla extract
- 1/2 tsp baking powder
- 2 tbsp swerve confectioners sweetener or monkfruit
- 1/4 tsp Xanthan powder
- Whipped Cream Vanilla Frosting Ingredients:
- 1/2 cup heavy whipping cream
- 2 tbs 2 tbsp swerve confectioners sweetener or monkfruit
- 1/2 tsp vanilla extract

Directions:

1. Preheat the mini waffle maker.
2. In a medium-size blender, add all of the chaffle cake ingredients and blend it on high until it's smooth and creamy. Allow the batter to sit for just a minute. It may seem a bit watery but it will work just fine.
3. Add about 2 to 3 tablespoons of batter to your waffle maker and cook it for about 2 to 3 minutes until it's golden brown.
4. In a separate bowl, start making the whipped cream vanilla frosting.
5. Add all of the ingredients and mix it with a hand mixer until the whipping cream is thick and forms soft peaks.
6. Allow the keto birthday cake chaffles to cool completely before frosting your cake. If you frost it too soon, it will melt the frosting.
7. Enjoy!

Keto Italian Cream Chaffle Cake Recipe

Ingredients:

- Sweet Chaffle Ingredients:
- 4 oz Cream Cheese softened and room temp
- 4 eggs
- 1 tablespoon melted butter
- 1 teaspoon vanilla extract
- 1/2 teaspoon cinnamon
- 1 tablespoon monkfruit sweetener or your favorite keto-approved sweetener
- 4 tablespoons coconut flour
- 1 tablespoon almond flour
- 1 1/2 teaspoons baking powder
- 1 tbs coconut shredded and unsweetened
- 1 tbs walnuts chopped

- Italian Cream Frosting Ingredients:

- 2 oz cream cheese softened and room temp

- 2 tbs butter room temp

- 2 tbs monkfruit sweetener or your favorite keto-approved sweetener

- 1/2 teaspoon vanilla

Directions:

1. In a medium-size blender, add the cream cheese, eggs, melted butter, vanilla, sweetener, coconut flour, almond flour, and baking powder. Optional: Add the shredded coconut and walnuts to the mixture or save it for the frosting. Either way is great!

2. Blend the ingredients on high until it's smooth and creamy.

3. Preheat the mini waffle maker.

4. Add the ingredients to the preheated waffle maker.

5. Cook for about 2 to 3 minutes until the waffles are done.

6. Remove and allow the chaffles to cool.

7. In a separate bowl, start to make the frosting by adding all the ingredients together. Stir until it's smooth and creamy.

8. Once the chaffles have completely cool, frost the cake.

NOTES

Makes 8 mini chaffles or 3 to 4 large chaffles.

Keto Peanut Butter Chaffle Cake Recipe

Servings:4

Ingredients:

- Peanut Butter Chaffle Ingredients:

- 2 Tbs Sugar Free Peanut Butter Powder

- 2 Tbs Monkfruit Confectioner's

- 1 egg

- 1/4 Tsp Baking Powder

- 1 Tbs heavy whipping cream

- 1/4 tsp Peanut Butter extract

- Peanut Butter Frosting Ingredients:

- 2 Tbs Monkfruit Confectioners

- 1 Tbs Butter softened and room temp

- 1 tbs sugar free natural peanut butter or peanut butter powder

- 2 Tbs Cream Cheese softened and room temp

- 1/4 tsp vanilla

Directions:

1. In a small bowl, whip up the egg.

2. Add the remaining ingredients and mix well until the batter is smooth and creamy.

3. If you don't have the peanut butter extract, you can skip it. It does add a more intense peanut butter flavor that is absolutely wonderful and makes this extract worth investing in.

4. Pour half the batter in a mini waffle maker and cook it for 2 to 3 minutes until it's fully cooked.

5. In a separate small bowl, add the sweetener, cream cheese, sugar free natural peanut butter, and vanilla. Mix the frosting until everything is well incorporated.

6. Spread the frosting on the waffle cake after it has completely cooled down to room temperature.

7. Or you can pipe the frosting too!

8. Or you can heat the frosting and add a 1/2 teaspoon of water to make it a peanut butter glaze you can drizzle on your peanut butter chaffle too! We like it either way!

Easy Soft Cinnamon Rolls Chaffle Cake

Servings:2

Ingredients:

- 1 egg

- 1/2 cup mozzarella cheese

- 1/2 tsp vanilla

- 1/2 tsp cinnamon

- 1 tbs monk fruit confectioners blend

Directions:

1. Preheat dash mini waffle maker.

2. In a small bowl, whip the egg.

3. Add the remaining ingredients.

4. Spray the waffle maker with non-stick cooking spray.

5. Makes 2 chaffles.

6. Divide mixture.

7. Cook half the mixture for about 4 minutes or until golden brown.

NOTES

Optional Glaze: 1 tbs cream cheese warmed in the microwave for 15 seconds, and 1 tbs monk fruit confectioners blend. Mix and spread over the warm chaffle.

Optional Frosting: 1 tbs cream cheese (room temp), 1 tbs room temp butter (room temp), and 1 tbs mmonk fruit confectioners blend. Mix all ingredients together and spread on top of the chaffle.

Top with optional frosting, glaze, nuts, sugar-free syrup, whipped cream or simply dust with monk fruit confectioners sugar.

Lemon Cake Chaffles

Servings:2

Cooking Time: 6 Minutes

Ingredients:

- 1 tbsp Coconut Flour

- 4 tsp Sweetener sugar alternative or preferred sweetener

- 1/4 tsp Baking Powder

- 1 Egg room temp

- 1 oz Cream Cheese room temp

- 1/2 tsp Lemon Extract

- 1/2 tsp Vanilla Extract

Directions:

1. Gather all the ingredients. Note – For quick room temperature eggs, submerge egg in warm water for 3-5 min. For quick room temperature cream cheese, take the amount needed and microwave for 10-15 sec.
2. Plug-in Dash Mini Waffle Maker to pre-heat.
3. In a small mixing bowl, add Coconut Flour, sweetener, Baking Powder and mix.
4. Next, add egg, cream cheese, Lemon Extract, Vanilla Extract and mix with a whisk until well combined.
5. Pour batter into waffle iron and cook for 3-4 min until browned to liking. Enjoy with your favorite sugar-free syrup or just as is!

Almond Joy Cake Chaffle Recipe

Servings:6

Ingredients:

- Chocolate Chaffles:
- 1 egg
- 1 ounce cream cheese
- 1 tablespoon almond flour
- 1 tablespoon unsweetened cocoa powder
- 1 tablespoon erythritol sweetener blend
- 1/2 teaspoon vanilla extract
- 1/4 teaspoon instant coffee powder
- Coconut Filling:
- 1 1/2 teaspoons coconut oil melted
- 1 tablespoon heavy cream
- 1/4 cup unsweetened finely shredded coconut
- 2 ounces cream cheese
- 1 tablespoon confectioner's sweetener
- 1/4 teaspoon vanilla extract
- 14 whole almonds

Directions:

1. For the Chaffles:
2. Preheat mini Dash waffle iron until thoroughly hot.
3. In a medium bowl, whisk all chaffle ingredients together until well combined.
4. Pour half of the batter into waffle iron.
5. Close and cook 3-5 minutes, until done. Remove to a wire rack.
6. Repeat for the second chaffle.
7. For the Filling:
8. Soften cream to room temperature or warm in the microwave for 10 seconds.
9. Add all ingredients to a bowl and mix until smooth and well-combined.
10. Assembly:
11. Spread half the filling on one chaffle and place 7 almonds evenly on top of the filling.
12. Repeat with the second chaffle and stack together.

Pecan Pie Chaffle Cake

Ingredients:

- PECAN PIE FILLING Ingredients:
- 2 T butter softened
- 1 T Sukrin Gold
- 1/8 tsp blackstrap molasses optional but helps with color and flavor
- 2 T Maple Bourbon Pecan Skinny Syrup
- 2 T heavy whipping cream
- 2 large egg yolks
- Pinch salt
- 2 T pecans lightly toasted (I did it in the Airfryer)
- PECAN PIE CHAFFLE Ingredients:
- 1 egg
- 1 T heavy whipping cream
- 2 T cream cheese softened
- 1/2 tsp maple extract Olive Nation
- 3 T almond flour
- 1 T oat fiber or another T almond flour
- 1 T Sukrin Gold
- 1/2 tsp baking powder
- 2 T pecans chopped

Directions:

1. PECAN PIE FILLING Directions:
2. Add butter, sweetener, heavy whipping cream and syrups to a small saucepan on low heat.
3. Whisk until well combined.
4. Remove from heat.
5. Pour 1/2 of the mixture into egg yolks and whisk well.
6. Add that mixture back into the saucepan while stirring continuously.
7. Add a pinch of salt and pecan.
8. Let simmer until it starts to thicken. Remove from heat and let cool while making the Chaffles.
9. PECAN PIE CHAFFLE CAKE Directions:
10. Mix all ingredients except pecans in a small blender for about 15 seconds. Stop and scrape down the sides with a spatula, and continue mixing for another 15 seconds until well blended. Mix in pecans with a spatula. Pour 3 T of batter in preheated mini waffle maker. Cook for 1 1/2 mins. Remove to cooling rack. Repeat. Will make 3 full Chaffles with a tiny one for tasting!
11. Put 1/3 of the pecan pie filling on each Chaffle and assemble as desired!

Carrot Chaffle Cake Recipe

Servings:6

Ingredients:

- Carrot Chaffle Cake Ingredients:
- 1/2 cup carrot shredded
- 1 egg
- 2 T butter melted
- 2 T heavy whipping cream
- 3/4 cup almond flour
- 1 T walnuts chopped

- 2 T powdered sweetener
- 2 tsp cinnamon
- 1 tsp pumpkin spice
- 1 tsp baking powder
- Cream Cheese Frosting
- 4 oz cream cheese softened
- 1/4 cup powdered sweetener
- 1 tsp vanilla extract
- 1-2 T heavy whipping cream depending on the consistency you prefer

Directions:

1. Mix your dry ingredients - almond flour, cinnamon, pumpkin spice, baking powder, powdered sweetener, and walnut pieces.

2. Add the wet ingredients- grated carrot, egg, melted butter, heavy cream.

3. Add 3 T batter to preheated mini waffle maker. Cook 2 1/2 - 3 minutes.

4. Mix frosting ingredients together with a hand mixer with whisk attachment until well combined.

5. Stack waffles and add frosting between each layer!

Cap'n Crunch Cereal Chaffle Cake

Servings:2

Ingredients:

- 1 egg
- 2 tablespoons almond flour
- 1/2 teaspoon coconut flour
- 1 tablespoon butter melted
- 1 tablespoon cream cheese room temp
- 20 drops Captain Cereal flavoring
- 1/4 teaspoon vanilla extract
- 1/4 teaspoon baking powder
- 1 tablespoon confectioners sweetener
- 1/8 teaspoon xanthan gum

Directions:

1. Preheat the mini waffle maker.

2. Mix or blend all of the ingredients until smooth and creamy. Allow the batter to rest for a few minutes for the flour to absorb the liquid.

3. Add about 2 to 3 tablespoons of batter to your waffle maker and cook it for about 2 1/2 minutes.

4. Top with fresh whipped cream (I added 10 drops of Captain cereal flavorinand syrup!

German Chocolate Chaffle Cake Recipe

Servings:4

Ingredients:

- German Chocolate Chaffle Cake Ingredients:
- 2 eggs
- 1 tablespoon melted butter
- 1 tablespoon cream cheese softened to room temperature
- 2 tablespoons unsweetened cocoa powder or unsweetened raw cacao powder
- 2 tablespoons almond flour
- 2 teaspoons coconut flour
- 2 tablespoons Pyure granulated sweetener blend
- 1/2 teaspoon baking powder
- 1/2 teaspoon instant coffee granules dissolved in 1 tablespoon hot water
- 1/2 teaspoon vanilla extract
- 2 pinches salt
- German Chocolate Chaffle Cake Filling Ingredients:
- 1 egg yolk
- 1/4 cup heavy cream
- 2 tablespoons Pyure granulated sweetener blend
- 1 tablespoon butter
- 1/2 teaspoon caramel or maple extract
- 1/4 cup chopped pecans
- 1/4 cup unsweetened flaked coconut
- 1 teaspoon coconut flour

Directions:

1. Chaffle Directions:
2. Preheat mini Dash waffle iron until thoroughly hot.
3. In a medium bowl, whisk all ingredients together until well combined.
4. Spoon a heaping 2 tablespoons of batter into waffle iron, close and cook 3-5 minutes, until done.
5. Remove to a wire rack.
6. Repeat 3 times.
7. Filling Directions:
8. In a small saucepan over medium heat, combine the egg yolk, heavy cream, butter, and sweetener.
9. Simmer slowly, stirring constantly for 5 minutes.
10. Remove from heat and stir in extract, pecans, flaked coconut, and coconut flour.

NOTES

Assembly: Spread one-third of the filling in between each of 2 layers of chaffles and the remaining third on top chaffle and serve.

Halloween Monster Chocolate Chaffle Cake Recipe

Ingredients:

- Chaffle Ingredients:
- 2 eggs lg
- 2 T Special dark cocoa
- 2 T Swerve Confectioners
- 4 T cream cheese softened
- 2 T Mayo
- 2 T almond flour
- 1/2 tsp baking powder
- 1/2 tsp espresso powder
- 1/8 tsp salt
- 2 tsp Vanilla extract
- Whipped Cream Frosting (Stabilized) Ingredients:
- 2 tsp unflavored gelatin
- 4 tsp Cold Water
- 1 Cup heavy whipping cream
- 2 T Swerve Confectioners
- 1/2 tsp vanilla extract

Directions:

1. Chaffle Directions:
2. Mix all ingredients in a small blender.
3. Put 3 tablespoons of batter in preheated mini waffle maker and cook 2 1/2-3 minutes.
4. Repeat.
5. Halloween Monster Chocolate Chaffle Cake
6. Place your beaters and your mixing bowl in the freezer for about 15 minutes to allow them to cool.
7. In a microwave-safe bowl, sprinkle the gelatin over the cold water. Stir, and allow to "bloom". This takes about 5 minutes.
8. Microwave the gelatin mixture for 10 seconds. It will become a liquid. Stir to make sure everything is dissolved.
9. In your chilled mixing bowl, begin whipping the cream on a low speed. Add in the confectioners sweetener.
10. Move to a higher speed and watch for good peaks to begin to form.
11. Once the whipping cream is starting to peak, switch back to a lower speed and slowly drizzle the melted liquid gelatin mixture in. Once it's in, switch back to a higher speed and continue to beat until it's reached stiff peaks.
12. Place in piping bags and pipe on your cake.

NOTES

Monsters and filling are made with stabilized whipped cream and food coloring. Candy eyes are for decoration purposes only and are not sugar-free.

BREAKFAST CHAFFLES RECIPES

Keto Blt Chaffle Sandwich

Servings:1

Ingredients:

- Chaffle bread Ingredients:
- 1/2 cup mozzarella shredded
- 1 egg
- 1 tbs green onion diced
- 1/2 tsp Italian seasoning
- Sandwich Ingredients:
- Bacon pre-cooked
- Lettuce
- Tomato sliced
- 1 tbs mayo

Directions:

1. Preheat the mini waffle maker

2. In a small bowl, whip the egg.

3. Add the cheese, seasonings, and onion. Mix it until it's well incorporated.

4. Place half the batter in the mini waffle maker and cook it for 4 minutes.

5. If you want a crunchy bread, add a tsp of shredded cheese to the mini waffle iron for 30 seconds before adding the batter. The extra cheese on the outside creates the best crust!

6. After the first chaffle is complete, add the remaining batter to the mini waffle maker and cook it for 4 minutes.

7. Add the mayo, bacon, lettuce, and tomato to your sandwich.

8. Enjoy!

NOTES

OMG! It was absolutely delicious!

Open-faced Keto French Dip Sandwich With A Chaffle

Servings:2

Cooking Time: 12 Minutes

Ingredients:

- 1 egg white
- 1/4 cup mozzarella cheese, shredded (packed)
- 1/4 cup sharp cheddar cheese, shredded (packed)
- 3/4 tsp water
- 1 tsp coconut flour
- 1/4 tsp baking powder
- pinch of salt

Directions:

1. Preheat the oven to 425 degrees. Plug the Dash Mini Waffle Maker in the wall and grease lightly once it is hot.

2. Combine all of the ingredients in a bowl and stir to combine.

3. Spoon 1/2 of the batter on the waffle maker and close the lid. Set a timer for 4 minutes, and do not lift the top until the cooking time is complete. Lifting beforehand can cause the Chaffle keto

sandwich recipe to separate and stick to the waffle iron. It is essential to let it cook for the entire 4 minutes before lifting the lid.

4. Remove the chaffle from the waffle iron and set it aside. Repeat the same steps above with the rest of the chaffle batter.

5. Cover a cookie sheet with parchment paper and place chaffles a few inches apart.

6. Add 1/4 to 1/3 cup of the slow cooker keto roast beef from the following recipe. Drain the excess broth/gravy before adding it to the top of the chaffle.

7. Add a slice of deli cheese or shredded cheese on top. Swiss and provolone are both great options.

8. Place on the top rack of the oven for 5 minutes so that the cheese can melt. If you'd like the cheese to bubble and begin to brown, turn the oven to broil for 1 min. (The swiss cheese may not brown)

9. Enjoy open-faced with a small bowl of beef broth for dipping.

Notes

The nutritional information provided is only for the chaffles sandwich keto recipe. It does not include the beef or added cheese on top of the sandwich. That info will vary depending on the cut of beef you use and type of cheese.

Halloween Spiced Ghost Pancakes Recipe

Ingredients:

- 2 eggs
- 2 oz Cream Cheese softened
- 1/2 tsp vanilla extract
- 1 1/2 tsp apple pie spice
- 1/2 T sweetener
- 1/4 cup + 2 T almond flour
- 1/4 tsp baking powder

Directions:

1. Mix everything together in a small blender.

2. Let batter rest for 5 minutes.

3. Put 3 tablespoons of batter in preheated mini griddle.

4. Cook for 1 1/2 minutes.

5. Flip and cook for another 1 1/2 min.

6. Ghost is whipped cream that I piped into ghost.

7. Add mini chocolate chips for eyes and mouth.

8. Freeze overnight.

Garlic Bread Chaffle

Servings:2

Cooking Time: 10 Minutes

Ingredients:

- 1 large egg
- 1/2 cup finely shredded mozzarella
- 1 teaspoon coconut flour
- ¼ teaspoon baking powder
- ½ teaspoon garlic powder
- 1 tablespoon butter, melted
- 1/4 teaspoon garlic salt
- 2 tablespoons Parmesan
- 1 teaspoon minced parsley

Directions:

1. Plug in your mini waffle iron to preheat. Preheat oven to 375 degrees.

2. Add the egg, mozzarella, coconut flour, baking powder, and garlic powder to a mixing bowl and whisk well to combine.

3. Pour half of the chaffle batter into the waffle iron and cook for 3 minutes or until the steam stops. Place the chaffle on a baking sheet.

4. Repeat with the remaining chaffle batter.

5. Stir together the butter and garlic salt and brush over the chaffles.

6. Top the chaffles with the Parmesan.

7. Place the pan in the oven for 5 minutes to melt the cheese.

8. Sprinkle with parsley before serving.

Notes

The garlic salt does make these a bit salty - feel free to swap in fresh minced garlic or garlic powder, if you're watching salt.

Jicama Hash Brown Chaffle Recipe

Servings:4

Ingredients:

- 1 large jicama root
- 1/2 medium onion minced
- 2 garlic cloves pressed
- 1 cup cheese of choice I used Halloumi
- 2 eggs whisked
- Salt and Pepper

Directions:

1. Peel jicama

2. Shred in food processor

3. Place shredded jicama in large colander, sprinkle with 1-2 tsp of salt. Mix well and allow to drain.

4. Squeeze out as much liquid as possible (very important step)

5. Microwave for 5-8 minutes

6. Mix all ingredients together

7. Sprinkle a little cheese on waffle iron before adding 3 T of mixture, sprinkle a little more cheese on top of mixture

NOTES

Top with a sunny side up egg!

We precook the jicama in the microwave to get is soft. You can find jicama at your local grocery store or even at Walmart!

If you haven't experienced jicama in your dining repertoire, you have everything to gain — and if you're hoping to shed some excess pounds, this might be your new favorite.

Easy Corndog Chaffle Recipe

Servings:5

Ingredients:

- 2 eggs
- 1 cup Mexican cheese blend
- 1 tbs almond flour
- 1/2 tsp cornbread extract
- 1/4 tsp salt
- hot dogs with hot dog sticks

Directions:

1. Preheat corndog waffle maker.
2. In a small bowl, whip the eggs.
3. Add the remaining ingredients except the hotdogs
4. Spray the corndog waffle maker with non-stick cooking spray.
5. Fill the corndog waffle maker with the batter halfway filled.
6. Place a stick in the hot dog.
7. Place the hot dog in the batter and slightly press down.
8. Spread a small amount of better on top of the hot dog, just enough to fill it.
9. Makes about 4 to 5 chaffle corndogs
10. Cook the corndog chaffles for about 4 minutes or until golden brown.
11. When done, they will easily remove from the corndog waffle maker with a pair of tongs.
12. Serve with mustard, mayo, or sugar free ketchup!

Avocado Toast Chaffle Recipe

Servings:2

Ingredients:

- 1/2 cup mozzarella cheese shredded
- 1 egg
- Pinch of salt
- 1/2 avocado mashed into guacamole and spread over the chaffle

Directions:

1. Preheat mini waffle iron. We use the Dash mini waffle iron.
2. In a small bowl, whip the egg.
3. Add the remaining ingredients and mix until fully combined.
4. Add 1/2 the mixture to the mini waffle maker and cook for about 3 to 4 minutes until it's done and golden brown.
5. Serve warm and enjoy.

Low Carb Reuben Chaffle Sandwich Recipe

Servings:2

Ingredients:

- Rye Bread Chaffle Ingredients:
- 1 egg
- 2 tablespoons almond flour
- 1 tablespoon melted butter
- 1 tablespoon mozzarella cheese
- pinch salt
- pinch garlic powder
- 1/2 teaspoon baking powder
- 1/2 teaspoon of caraway seeds
- Reuben Sandwich Ingredients:
- 2 tablespoons of sauerkraut
- 2 slices of swiss cheese
- 1-2 ounces thinly sliced corned beef or pastrami
- Russian Sauce Ingredients:
- 1 tablespoon mayo
- 1 teaspoon sugar-free ketchup
- 1 teaspoon dill relish
- pinch of monk fruit sweetener

Directions:

1. Preheat mini waffle maker.
2. Mix all rye bread chaffle ingredients in a small bowl.
3. Cook chaffles for 4 minutes in the mini waffle maker.
4. Mix together sauce ingredients in a small bowl.
5. Layer sandwich together and enjoy!

Easy Turkey Burger With Halloumi Cheese Chaffle Recipe

Servings:4

Ingredients:

- 1 lb Ground Turkey raw (no need to precook the turkey)
- 8 oz Halloumi shredded
- 1 zucchini medium, shredded
- 2 tbsp Chives chopped
- 1/2 tsp Salt
- 1/4 tsp Pepper

Directions:

1. Add all ingredients to a bowl mix thoroughly together.
2. Shape into 8 evenly sized patties
3. Preheat mini griddle.
4. Cook the patties 5-7 minutes

Keto Fluffernutter Sandwich Recipe

Servings:2

Ingredients:

- Chaffle Sandwich Bread Ingredients:
- 1 tablespoon almond flour
- 1 teaspoon water
- 1 tablespoon Dukes mayonnaise
- 1/8 teaspoon baking powder
- 1 egg
- Pinch of pink Himalayan salt

- Keto Marshmallow Fluff Ingredients:
- 1 cup liquid allulose sweetener
- 1 teaspoon vanilla extract
- 1/4 cup water
- 1 packet of Knox unflavored gelatin
- Additional Filling Ingredients:
- Sugar Free Peanut Butter

Directions:

1. Chaffle Sandwich Bread Directions:
2. Mix all the ingredients together in a small bowl.
3. Pour half the batter into a mini dash waffle maker and cook for about 3 1/2 to 4 minutes or until golden brown.
4. Set aside to cool.
5. Keto Marshmallow Fluff
6. In a small bowl, add the water.
7. Sprinkle the packet of unflavored gelatin over the water and let it set for about 2 minutes. Give it a little stir to help combine all the gelatin if needed.
8. Using a stand mixer, add the prepared gelatin, vanilla extract, and liquid allulose to the bowl.
9. Add the whisk attachment.
10. Turn on the mixer to level 2 (slow) until the whisk begins to move.
11. Once the mixture has begun to move, turn the mixer speed all the way up to level 10. I used the splash guard on my mixer but you may not need to if your bowl is deep enough.
12. Set a timer for exactly 20 minutes. You will see the liquid start to get texture at the 10-minute mark but to make it extra fluffy go the full 20 minutes.
13. Set aside when complete.
14. Assembly
15. After the chaffles and marshmallow fluff are made. Take one of the chaffle sandwich bread pieces and layer a good amount of sugar-free peanut butter on it.
16. Next, add a dollop of marshmallow fluff to the peanut butter layer.
17. Top with the second chaffle sandwich bread and enjoy! Your taste buds will thank you later!

NOTES

Almond Flour Chaffle Sandwich Bread **Notes**

Takes between 3 and 4 minutes to cook.

Tastes more eggy than the coconut flour version.

The almond flour version tends to be a bit thinner than the coconut wonder bread recipe.

Reheats nicely in the air fryer, toaster, or toaster oven.

Add them to a freezer-friendly ziplock bag or container in between parchment paper to freeze them for later too.

Chocolate Chip Cannoli Chaffle Recipe

Ingredients:

- Chocolate Chip Chaffle Ingredients:
- 1 T Butter melted
- 1 T Golden Monkfruit sweetener
- 1 Egg Yolk
- 1/8 tsp Vanilla Extract
- 3 T Almond Flour
- 1/8 tsp Baking Powder
- 1 T Chocolate Chips sugar free
- Cannoli Topping Ingredients:
- 2 oz Cream Cheese
- 2 T Confectioners Sweetener Low Carb
- 6 T Ricotta full fat
- 1/4 tsp Vanilla Extract
- 5 drops Lemon Extract

Directions:

1. Preheat the mini waffle maker.
2. In a small bowl, mix together all of the chaffle ingredients.
3. Place half of the ingredients in the mini waffle maker.
4. Cook the chaffle for about 3 to 4 minutes.
5. While the chaffle is cooking start making the Cannoli topping.
6. Add all of the ingredients for the Cannoli topping in a blender and blend everything together until it's smooth and creamy.

Zucchini Nut Bread Chaffle Recipe

Servings:4

Ingredients:

- 1 cup shredded zucchini approximately 1 small zucchini
- 1 egg
- 1/2 teaspoon cinnamon
- 1 Tbsp plus 1 tsp erythritol blend
- Dash ground nutmeg
- 2 tsp melted butter
- 1 ounce softened cream cheese
- 2 tsp coconut flour
- 1/2 tsp baking powder
- 3 tablespoons chopped walnuts or pecans
- Frosting Ingredients:
- 2 ounces cream cheese at room temperature
- 2 Tbsp butter at room temperature
- 1/4 tsp cinnamon
- 2 Tbsp caramel sugar-free syrup , OR 1 Tbsp confectioner's sweetener, such as Swerve plus 1/8 tsp caramel extract
- 1 Tbsp chopped walnuts or pecans

Directions:

1. Grate zucchini and place in a colander over a plate to drain for 15 minutes. With your hands, squeeze out as much moisture as possible.
2. Preheat mini Dash waffle iron until thoroughly hot.

3. In a medium bowl, whisk all chaffle ingredients together until well combined.

4. Spoon a heaping 2 tablespoons of batter into waffle iron, close and cook 3-5 minutes, until done.

5. Remove to a wire rack. Repeat 3 times.

6. Frosting

7. Mix all ingredients together until smooth and spread over each chaffle.

8. Top with additional chopped nuts.

Jalapeno Popper Grilled Cheese Chaffle Recipe

Ingredients:

- 2 Jalapenos sliced lengthwise seeds and membranes removed
- 4 ounces cream cheese
- 4 slices bacon crispy cooked
- 2 slices Monterey jack
- 2 slices sharp cheddar
- Chaffle Ingredients:
- 2 eggs
- 1 cup mozzarella shredded

Directions:

1. Fill each jalapeno half with approximately 1 ounce of cream cheese.

2. Bake stuffed jalapenos in a preheated Air fryer for 10 minutes at 350*.

3. Build your sandwiches: Place 1 slice each Monterey Jack on 2 Chaffles, add 2 jalapeño halves to each, 2 slices of bacon, then cheddar cheese. Top with the other 2 Chaffles.

4. Butter each side of the sandwiches. Grill each side until lightly browned.

NOTES

TIP: Use gloves to cut the peppers and remove the seeds. Wash hands thoroughly after working with them as they can be an irritant if you touch your face or eyes.

Okra Fritter Chaffles Recipe

Servings:4

Ingredients:

- 1 egg
- 1 Tbsp mayo
- 2 Tbsp heavy cream
- 1/2 Tbsp Tony Chachere's Creole Seasoning
- Onion powder
- Salt and pepper to taste
- 1/4 cup almond flour
- 1 cup okra fresh or frozen, thawed
- 1/4 cup mozzarella shredded

Directions:

1. Whip together egg, mayo, heavy cream, and seasoning.

2. Add almond flour.

3. Combine well and let batter rest for 5 -10 minutes.

4. Stir in okra.

5. Add 3 tablespoons of batter to preheated waffle maker or griddle.

6. Put a little shredded mozzarella on the griddle before adding batter and a little on top after adding it.

7. Cook for 5 mins.

8. Flip and cook a couple more minutes until it reaches your desired crispiness.

9. Remove to a cooling rack and sprinkle with sea salt.

Big Mac Chaffle

Servings:1

Cooking Time: 10 Minutes

Ingredients:

- For the cheeseburgers:
- 1/3 pound ground beef
- 1/2 teaspoon garlic salt
- 2 slices American cheese
- For the Chaffles:
- 1 large egg
- 1/2 cup finely shredded mozzarella
- 1/4 teaspoon garlic salt
- For the Big Mac Sauce:
- 2 teaspoons mayonnaise
- 1 teaspoon ketchup
- 1 teaspoon dill pickle relish
- splash vinegar to taste
- To assemble:
- 2 tablespoons shredded lettuce
- 3-4 dill pickles
- 2 teaspoons minced onion

Directions:

1. To make the burgers:

2. Heat a griddle over medium high heat.

3. Divide the ground beef into 2 equal sized balls and place each on the griddle, at least 6 inches apart.

4. Let cook for 1 minute.

5. Use a small salad plate to firmly press straight down on the balls of beef to flatten. Sprinkle with garlic salt.

6. Cook 2 minutes or until halfway cooked through. Flip the burgers carefully and sprinkle with remaining garlic salt.

7. Continue cooking 2 minutes or until cooked through.

8. Place one slice of cheese over each patty and then stack the patties and set aside on a plate. Cover with foil.

9. To make the chaffles:

10. Heat the mini waffle iron and spray with non-stick spray.

11. Whisk together the egg, cheese, and garlic salt until well combined.

12. Add half of the egg mixture to the waffle iron and cook for 2-3 minutes. Set aside and repeat with remaining batter.

13. To make the Big Mac Sauce:

14. Whisk together all ingredients.

15. To assemble burgers:

16. Top one chaffle with the stacked burger patties, shredded lettuce, pickles, and onions.

17. Spread the Big Mac sauce over the other chaffle and place sauce side down over the sandwich.

18. Eat immediately.

19. TIPS & NOTES:

20. Feel free to double or quadruple this recipe.

21. I find it easiest to make the Big Mac sauce in advance and then cook the chaffles while the burgers are cooking. This looks like a lot of steps, but all goes very quickly.

Taco Chaffle Recipe

Servings:4

Cooking Time: 15 Minutes

Ingredients:

- 1 pound ground beef (80/20)
- 1 recipe or packet taco seasoning mix
- ½ cup water (if using a store-bought packet use their specified amount of water)
- 4 large eggs
- 2 cups freshly grated cheese (cheddar, mozzarella, monterey jack, or pepper jack cheese are all fine)
- 1 teaspoon chili powder
- ½ teaspoon cumin
- optional toppings: shredded cheese, sour cream, salsa, green onion, olives, tomato, lettuce, avocado slices, fresh cilantro.

Directions:

1. Make Taco Meat

2. Brown ground beef, add copy cat taco seasoning mix, and water. Cook until water evaporates and taco meat is to your desired thickness, about 10 minutes. Keep warm until ready to use. (Note: if using a store bought taco seasoning packet, follow their instructions for making taco meat.)

3. Make The Chaffle

4. Preheat waffle iron to the highest setting.

5. In a small bowl add grated cheese and mix well.

6. Pour mixture over the center of the hot waffle maker and close lid.

7. Cook until the outside is to your desired crispiness. Repeat for each taco shell. Keep warm in an oven or air fryer until ready to use.

8. Assemble The Tacos

9. Fill the cooked keto chaffles with the taco meat and then your favorite taco toppings.

NOTES

Don't miss all of our helpful hints, substitution ideas, cooking tips

VARIATIONS: use our Mexican ground beef recipe for added flavor. add cayenne pepper to the batter for extra spice. Use cheddar, jack, pepper jack, or mozzarella. Add chopped fresh cilantro or finely chopped chives to the batter. Use ground chicken or turkey instead of beef.

SERVING SUGGESTIONS: Top with your favorite taco toppings.

NOTE: if using a mini waffle iron this recipe will make 2 chaffles. If using a standard waffle iron, this will make one.

Apple Pie Churro Chaffle Tacos Recipe

Ingredients:

- Chayote Apple Pie Filling
- 1 Chayote Squash cooked, peeled and sliced
- 1 T Kerrygold butter melted
- 2 packets True Lemon
- 1/8 tsp cream of tartar
- 1/4 cup Swerve Brown
- 2 tsp Ceylon cinnamon powder more if you like
- 1/8 tsp ginger powder
- 1/8 tsp nutmeg
- Cinnamon Chaffle
- 2 eggs room temperature
- 1/4 cup mozzarella shredded
- 1 tsp Ceylon cinnamon
- 1 T Swerve Confectioners
- 2 tsp coconut flour
- 1/8 tsp baking powder
- 1 tsp vanilla extract

Directions:

1. How to make Apple Pie Taco Filling
2. Boil the whole chayote for 25 minutes. Let it cool. Peel and slice into 1/4 inch slices.
3. Mix all ingredients together and stir in chayote to coat well.
4. Place in a small baking dish and cover with foil. Bake for 20 minutes.
5. Place 1/4 of the mixture in a food processor or small blender and process until it reaches applesauce consistency.
6. Add to chayote slices and stir.
7. Apple Pie Churro Chaffle Taco Directions:
8. Whip eggs.
9. Add sweetener, cinnamon, and vanilla.
10. Mix well.
11. Add remaining ingredients and stir.
12. Put 3 T batter in preheated Dash Mini Griddle.
13. Cook for 5 minutes.
14. Sprinkle hot chaffle with cinnamon and granular sweetener mixture.
15. To Assemble
16. Place chaffles in taco holders or fold gently to shape.
17. Add 1/4 of Apple filling to each taco chaffle.
18. Top with whipped cream or vanilla bean ice cream.

Chickfila Copycat Chaffle Sandwich Recipe

Ingredients:

- 1 Chicken Breast
- 4 T of Dill Pickle Juice
- 2 T Parmesan Cheese powdered
- 2 T Pork Rinds ground
- 1 T Flax Seed ground
- Salt and Pepper
- 2 T Butter melted
- 1 Egg room temperature
- 1 Cup Mozzarella Cheese shredded
- 3 -5 drops of Stevia Glycerite
- 1/4 tsp Butter Extract

Directions:

1. Instructions For the Chicken:
2. Pound chicken to 1/2 inch thickness.
3. Cut in half and place in zip lock baggie with pickle
4. juice.
5. Seal baggie and place in the fridge for 1 hour to overnight.
6. Preheat Airfryer for 5 mins at 400*
7. In a small shallow bowl mix together Parmesan cheese, pork rinds, flaxseed, and S&P.
8. Remove chicken from the baggie and discard pickle juice.
9. Dip chicken in melted butter then in seasoning mix.
10. Place parchment paper round in Airfryer basket, brush the paper lightly with oil. (I used coconut)
11. Place chicken in preheated Airfryer and cook for 7 mins.
12. Flip chicken and Airfry for an additional 7-8 mins. (This can vary based on the size of your chickeInternal temp of 165*
13. Instructions For Chaffle Bun:
14. Mix everything together in a small bowl. Put 1/4 of the mixture in the preheated mini dash waffle iron. Cook for 4 mins. Remove to a cooking rack. Repeat x3
15. Assemble Sandwich's: Place rested chicken on one Chaffle bun, add 3 dill pickle slices. Cover with other buns. Repeat. Enjoy!

Dairy Free And Egg Free Chaffle Bread Recipe

Servings:2

Cooking Time: 3 Minutes

Ingredients:

- 3 tbsp almond flour
- 1 tbsp veganaise
- 1/8 tsp baking powder
- 1/4 cup ju.st egg an egg replacer

Directions:

1. Add all the ingredients to a small bowl and mix well until it's fully combined.
2. Preheat the mini Dash waffle maker and add half the mixture to the waffle maker.
3. Cook it for about 3 minutes.

4. Set on a cooling rack.

5. Cook the last bit of batter to make the second piece of bread.

NOTES

Perfect for sandwiches that are Low carb!

Dill Pickle Egg Salad Sandwiches

Servings:3

Cooking Time: 20 Minutes

Ingredients:

- FOR THE EGG SALAD:
- 6 hard boiled eggs
- ½ cup chopped dill pickles
- 3 tablespoons mayonnaise
- 1 tablespoon prepared yellow mustard
- 1 tablespoon dill pickle juice
- 1 tablespoon fresh dill
- Salt and pepper, to taste
- FOR THE CHAFFLES:
- 3 eggs, beaten
- 1 tablespoon coconut flour
- 3/4 teaspoon baking powder
- 1 1/2 cups finely shredded mozzarella

Directions:

1. TO MAKE THE EGG SALAD:

2. Peel and chop the eggs into small pieces.

3. Add the eggs to a mixing bowl along with the remaining ingredients. Stir well to combine.

4. Eat immediately or store tightly covered in the fridge for up to 4 days.

5. TO MAKE THE CHAFFLES:

6. Plug in the waffle iron to preheat.

7. Whisk together the eggs, coconut flour, and baking powder. Stir in the mozzarella to combine.

8. Spoon just enough batter to cover the bottom of the waffle iron and close the waffle iron. Cook for 3 minutes. Remove the waffle and repeat with remaining batter until you have 6 chaffles cooked.

9. TO ASSEMBLE:

10. Divide the egg salad evenly between three chaffles.

11. Top with the remaining chaffles and serve.

Notes

If you'd prefer to use almond flour in place of coconut flour, increase the amount to 3 tablespoons.

Gingerbread Chaffles

Servings:4

Cooking Time: 16 Minutes

Ingredients:

- 1 cup mozzarella cheese shredded
- 2 tablespoons almond flour
- 1 tsp baking powder
- 2 eggs
- 1 tsp ground ginger
- 1/2 tsp cinnamon
- 1/4 tsp ground nutmeg
- 1/4 tsp ground cloves

- 2 tsp Swerve Sweetener

Directions:

1. Plugin your waffle maker.

2. In a medium bowl add in the mozzarella cheese, almond flour, baking powder, eggs, ginger, cinnamon, nutmeg, cloves, and swerve and mix well.

3. Add 1/4 of the keto Chaffle mix to the Dish Mini waffle maker at a time. Cook chaffle batter in the waffle maker for 4 minutes.

4. DO NOT open before the 4 minutes is up. It is VERY important that you do not open the waffle maker before the 4-minute mark. After that, you can open it to check it and make sure it is cooked all the way, but with these chaffles keeping the lid closed the whole time is VERY important.

5. When the first one is completely done cooking cook the next one.

6. Enjoy with some swerve confectioners sweetener or whipped cream on top.

Keto Sweet Bread Chaffle Recipe

Servings:1

Ingredients:

- 1 tbs almond flour
- 1 egg
- 1 tbs mayo
- 1/8 tsp baking powder
- 1 tbs Allulose sweetener powdered

- 1/4 tsp cinnamon
- 1/8 tsp salt

Directions:

1. Stir all ingredients together. Let rest for 5 min.

2. Stir again.

3. Preheat the mini waffle iron

4. Put half of dough in mini waffle maker.

5. Cook 3 minutes.

6. Repeat. Let cool.

Cheesy Garlic Bread Chaffle Recipe

Servings:2

Ingredients:

- Garlic Bread Chaffle Ingredients:
- 1/2 cup mozzarella cheese shredded
- 1 egg
- 1 tsp Italian seasoning
- 1/2 tsp garlic powder
- 1 tsp cream cheese I prefer to use flavored cream cheese such as chive and onion or jalapeno but you can use plain too
- Garlic Butter Topping Ingredients:
- 1 tbs butter
- 1/2 tsp Italian seasoning
- 1/2 tsp garlic powder
- Cheesy Bread Topping
- 2 tbs mozzarella cheese shredded
- dash of parsley or more Italian seasoning

Directions:

1. Preheat your mini waffle maker.

2. Preheat your oven to 350F.

3. In a small bowl, mix together all of the garlic bread chaffle ingredients until it's well combined.

4. Divide the mixture in half and cook the first chaffle for a minimum of 4 minutes. If you like you chaffles a bit crunchy on the outside, I would suggest you place a tsp of shredded cheese onto the waffle maker 30 seconds before adding the chaffle ingredients. This will create a nice, crunchy crust that's pretty amazing!

5. After you cook both of the garlic bread chaffles in the waffle maker, transfer them to a baking sheet.

6. In a separate small bowl, melt the butter in the microwave for about 10 seconds.

7. Add the garlic butter seasonings to the butter mixture.

8. Spread the butter mixture onto the warm chaffles with a basting brush.

9. Sprinkle a small amount of mozzarella on top of the garlic bread chaffles and then sprinkle with more Italian seasoning.

10. Bake for 5 minutes at 350F degrees. This is just enough time to melt the cheese on top of the Cheesy Garlic Bread Chaffles!

11. Serve warm and enjoy them with a sugar free marinara sauce such as Rao's marinara sauce!

NOTES

Serve warm and enjoy

Fried Pickle Chaffle Sticks

Servings:1

Ingredients:

- 1 egg large
- 1/4 cup pork panko
- 1/2 cup mozzarella
- 1 tablespoon pickle juice
- 6-8 thin pickle slices

Directions:

1. Mix together.
2. Add a thin layer to waffle iron.
3. Blot excess juice from pickles.
4. Add pickle slices and then another thin layer of mix.
5. Cook 4 minutes.

NOTES

Dipping Sauce: Ranch dressing mixed with Frank's hot sauce

Keto Wonder Bread Chaffle Recipe

Servings:2

Ingredients:

- 1 Tablespoons Almond Flour
- 1 Teaspoon Water
- 1 Tablespoon Dukes Mayonnaise
- 1/8 Teaspoon Baking Powder
- 1 egg
- Pinch of pink Himalayan salt

Directions:

1. Mix all the ingredients together in a small bowl. Pour half the batter into a mini dash waffle maker and cook for about 3 1/2 to 4 minutes or until golden brown.
2. Makes two mini wonder bread chaffles.

NOTES

Note: If you don't like mayonnaise, you can substitute it for 1 tablespoon of sour cream.

Corndog Chaffle Recipe

Ingredients:

- Flax Egg - Mix 1 T ground flaxseed with 3 T water
- Set aside to rest If you're not allergic to egg whites skip the flax and use 1 large egg
- 1 1/2 T Melted Butter
- 2 tsp sweetener granulated
- 3 T Almond Flour
- 1/4 tsp Baking Powder
- 1 Egg Yolk
- 2 T heaping Mexican Blend Cheese
- 1 T chopped Pickled Jalapeños
- 15 -20 drops Cornbread Flavoring
- Extra cheese for sprinkling on waffle maker

Directions:

1. Mix everything together. Let rest for 5 mins. Add 1 T of water or HWC if it's too thick.
2. Sprinkle shredded cheese on the bottom of the waffle maker. Add 1/3 of batter. Sprinkle top with more shredded cheese. Close waffle iron. Don't press down. Remove when cheese is crisp. Repeat. Makes 3.

NOTES

Flax Egg - Mix 1 T ground flaxseed with 3 T water Set aside to rest (If you're not allergic to egg whites skip the flax and use 1 large egg)

This is the cornbread flavoring I used.

Corn Silk (Zea Mays) Glycerite, Organic Dried Silk Alcohol-FREE Liquid Extract 2 oz

SAVORY CHAFFLE RECIPES

Halloumi Cheese Chaffle Recipe

Ingredients:

- 3 oz Halloumi cheese
- 2 T Pasta sauce optional

Directions:

1. Cut Halloumi cheese into 1/2 inch thick slices.
2. Place cheese in the UNHEATED waffle maker.
3. Turn waffle maker on.
4. Let it cook for about 3-6 minutes or until golden
5. brown and to your liking.
6. Let cool on a rack for a few minutes.
7. Add Low Carb marinara or pasta sauce.
8. Serve immediately. Enjoy!

Peanut Butter & Jelly Sammich Chaffle Recipe

Ingredients:

- Chaffle Ingredients:
- 2 eggs
- 1/4 cup mozzarella
- 1 tsp cinnamon
- 1 T Swerve Confectioners
- 2 tsp coconut flour
- 1/8 tsp baking powder
- 1 tsp vanilla extract
- Blueberry Compote Ingredients:
- 1 cup blueberries washed

- Zest of 1/2 lemon
- 1 T lemon juice freshly squeezed
- 1 T Swerve Confectioners
- 1/8 tsp xanthan gum
- 2 T water

Directions:

1. Blueberry Compote
2. Add everything except xanthan gum to small saucepan.
3. Bring to a boil, reduce heat and simmer for 5-10 minutes until it starts to thicken.
4. Sprinkle with xanthan gum and stir well.
5. Remove from heat and let cool.
6. Store in refrigerator until ready to use.

Blueberry & Brie Grilled Cheese Chaffle

Ingredients:

- Blueberry and Brie Grilled Cheese Ingredients:
- 2 Chaffles
- 1 T Blueberry Compote
- 1 oz Wisconsin Brie sliced thin
- 1 T Kerrygold butter
- CHAFFLE Ingredients:
- 1 egg beaten
- 1/4 cup mozzarella shredded
- 1 tsp Swerve confectioners
- 1 T cream cheese softened

- 1/4 tsp baking powder
- 1/2 tsp vanilla extract
- Blueberry Compote Ingredients:
- 1 cup blueberries washed
- Zest of 1/2 lemon
- 1 T lemon juice freshly squeezed
- 1 T Swerve Confectioners
- 1/8 tsp xanthan gum
- 2 T water

Directions:

1. Chaffle Directions:
2. Mix everything together.
3. Cook 1/2 batter for 2 1/2- 3 minutes in the mini waffle maker
4. Repeat.
5. Let cool slightly on a cooling rack.
6. Blueberry Compote Directions:
7. Add everything except xanthan gum to a small sauce pan. Bring to a boil, reduce heat and simmer for 5-10 minutes until it starts to thicken. Sprinkle with xanthan gum and stir well. Remove from heat and let cool. Store in refrigerator until ready to use.
8. Grilled Cheese Directions:
9. Heat butter in a small pan over medium heat. Place Brie slices on a Chaffle and top with generous 1 T scoop of prepared blueberry compote.
10. Place sandwich in pan and grill, flipping once until waffle is golden and cheese has melted, about 2 minutes per side.

Everything Bagel Chaffle Recipe

Servings:1

Cooking Time: 3 Minutes

Ingredients:

- 1 egg
- 1/2 cup sharp cheddar
- 1 tsp Everything Bagel seasoning

Directions:

1. In a small bowl, whip the egg till fluffy.
2. Add 1/2 cup sharp cheddar shredded cheese to the egg mixture and mix until it's fully combined.
3. Preheat the mini Dash waffle maker.
4. Once the mini waffle iron has been heated start making the chaffles.
5. For Crispy chaffles: add 1 tsp on shredded cheese to the hot waffle iron for 30 seconds before adding the egg batter mixture.
6. Pour half the mixture into the waffle iron.
7. Sprinkle the top of the mixture with the Everything Bagel Seasoning and close the lid.
8. Cook it for about 3 to 4 minutes or until the steam stops coming up from the waffle iron. Don't open the waffle iron before 3 minutes or else you will have a melted cheese gooey mess. The cheese needs to cook long enough to form a nice crust.

Banana Nut Chaffle Recipe

Servings:2

Ingredients:

- 1 egg
- 1 tbs cream cheese. softened and room temp
- 1 tbs sugar free cheesecake pudding optional ingredient because it is dirty keto
- 1/2 cup mozzarella cheese
- 1 tbs Monkfruit confectioners
- 1/4 tsp vanilla extract
- 1/4 tsp banana extract
- Optional Toppings:
- Sugar free caramel sauce
- Pecans

Directions:

1. Preheat the mini waffle maker
2. In a small bowl, whip the egg.
3. Add the remaining ingredients to the egg mixture and mix it until it's well incorporated.
4. Add half the batter to the waffle maker and cook it for a minimum of 4 minutes until it's golden brown.
5. Remove the finished chaffle and add the other half of the batter to cook the other chaffle.
6. Top with your optional ingredients and serve warm!
7. Enjoy!

Crispy Cheddar Chaffles Recipe

Servings:2

Ingredients:

- 1/2 cup shredded cheddar cheese (plus more for putting on the griddle)
- 1 tbsp almond flour
- 1 egg

Directions:

1. Preheat your waffle maker (a mini waffle maker works best but any waffle maker will work).
2. In a small bowl, whisk together the cheese, almond flour and egg until well combined.
3. Once your waffle maker is hot, evenly sprinkle a little cheddar cheese directly onto the griddle.
4. Pour half of the chaffle batter in and then sprinkle the top with more cheese; close the lid and cook for 2-3 minutes or until the automatic timer goes off. Repeat for next chaffle.

Recipe Notes

Feel free to flavor the chaffle batter to your liking with garlic powder, onion powder, diced jalapeños, Italian seasoning, cayenne or anything else you'd like.

Cranberry Swirl Chaffles With Orange Cream Cheese Frosting

Servings:6

Ingredients:

- Cranberry sauce:
- 1/2 cup cranberries fresh or frozen
- 2 Tbsp granulated erythritol
- 1/2 cup water
- 1/2 tsp vanilla extract
- Chaffles:
- 1 egg
- 1- ounce cream cheese at room temperature
- 1 Tbsp erythritol blend
- 1/2 tsp vanilla extract
- 1 tsp coconut flour
- 1/4 tsp baking powder
- Frosting:
- 1- ounce cream cheese at room temperature
- 1 Tbsp butter room temperature
- 1 Tbsp confectioner's sweetener
- 1/8 tsp orange extract OR 2 drops orange essential oil
- A few strands of grated orange zest for garnish optional

Directions:

1. For the cranberry swirl:
2. Combine the cranberries, water, and erythritol in a medium saucepan. Bring to a boil, then reduce heat to a gentle simmer.
3. Simmer for 10-15 minutes, until the cranberries pop and the sauce thickens.
4. Remove from heat and stir in the vanilla extract.
5. Mash the berries with the back of a spoon until a chunky sauce forms.
6. The sauce will thicken off the heat significantly.
7. For the chaffles:
8. Preheat mini Dash waffle iron until thoroughly hot.
9. In a medium bowl, whisk all chaffle ingredients together until well combined.
10. Spoon 2 tablespoons of batter into a waffle iron.
11. Add 1/2 of the cranberry sauce in little dollops over the batter of each chaffle.
12. Close and cook 3-5 minutes, until done. Remove to a wire rack.
13. Repeat for the second chaffle.
14. For the Frosting:
15. Mix all ingredients, except orange zest, together until smooth and spread over each chaffle.
16. Top with optional orange zest.

Everything Bagel Chaffles

Servings:2

Ingredients:

- 1 egg
- 1 tbsp almond flour
- 3/4 cup shredded mozzarella cheese (plus more for the griddle)
- 1 tsp Everything Bagel seasoning (plus more for topping)
- cream cheese (for topping)

Directions:

1. Preheat your mini waffle maker.
2. Mix the egg, almond flour, cheese and bagel seasoning together in a small bowl until well combined.
3. Once the waffle maker is hot, sprinkle a little shredded cheese directly onto the griddle and then pour HALF of your batter in. Sprinkle with more cheese and close the lid.
4. Cook until the automatic timer goes off or until it's crispy to your liking; repeat for next chaffle.
5. Let the chaffles cool for about a minute and then spread with cream cheese and top with more bagel seasoning. Enjoy!

Jicama Loaded Baked Potato Chaffle

Servings:4

Ingredients:

- 1 large jicama root
- 1/2 medium onion minced
- 2 garlic cloves pressed
- 1 cup cheese of choice I used Halloumi
- 2 eggs whisked
- Salt and Pepper

Directions:

1. Peel jicama and shred in food processor
2. Place shredded jicama in a large colander, sprinkle with 1-2 tsp of salt. Mix well and allow to drain.
3. Squeeze out as much liquid as possible (very important step)
4. Microwave for 5-8 minutes
5. Mix all ingredients together
6. Sprinkle a little cheese on waffle iron before adding 3 T of the mixture, sprinkle a little more cheese on top of the mixture
7. Cook for 5 minutes. Flip and cook 2 more.
8. Top with a dollop of sour cream, bacon pieces, cheese, and chives!

Biscuits And Gravy Chaffle Recipe

Servings:4

Ingredients:

- 2 tbs Unsalted Butter melted
- 2 Large Eggs
- 1 c. Mozzarella Cheese shredded
- 1 tbs Garlic minced
- 10 drops Cornbread Extract optional
- 1/2 tbs Lakanto Confectioners optional
- 1 tbs Almond Flour
- 1/4 tsp Granulated Onion
- 1/4 tsp Granulated Garlic
- 1 tsp Dried Parsley
- 1 tsp Baking Powder
- 1 batch Keto Sausage Biscuits and Gravy Recipe

Directions:

1. Preheat Mini Waffle Maker.
2. Melt the butter, let cool.
3. Whisk in the eggs, then fold in the shredded cheese.
4. Add the rest of ingredients and mix thoroughly.
5. Scoop 1/4 of batter onto waffle maker and cook 4 minutes.
6. Remove and let cool on wire rack.
7. Repeat for remaining 3 chaffles.

The Best Chaffle Recipe

Servings:2

Cooking Time: 3 Minutes

Ingredients:

- BASIC CHAFFLE RECIPE FOR SANDWICHES:
- 1/2 cup Mozzarella cheese (shredded)
- 1 large Egg
- 2 tbsp Wholesome Yum Blanched Almond Flour (or 2 tsp coconut flour)
- 1/2 tsp Psyllium husk powder (optional, but recommended for texture, sprinkle in so it doesn't clump)
- 1/4 tsp Baking powder (optional)
- GARLIC PARMESAN CHAFFLES:
- 1/2 cup Mozzarella cheese (shredded)
- 1/3 cup Grated Parmesan cheese
- 1 large Egg
- 1 clove Garlic (minced; or use 1/2 clove for milder garlic flavor)
- 1/2 tsp Italian seasoning
- 1/4 tsp Baking powder (optional)
- CINNAMON SUGAR (CHURRO) CHAFFLES:
- 1 large Egg
- 3/4 cup Mozzarella cheese (shredded)
- 2 tbsp Wholesome Yum Blanched Almond Flour (or 2 tsp coconut flour)
- 1 1/2 tbsp Unsalted butter (melted, divided, 1/2 tbsp for the batter + 1 tbsp for topping)

- 5 1/2 tbsp Besti Monk Fruit Allulose Blend (divided, 1 1/2 tbsp for the batter + 1/4 cup for topping)
- 1 1/4 tsp Cinnamon (divided, 1/2 tsp for the batter + 3/4 tsp for topping)
- 1/2 tsp Vanilla extract
- 1/2 tsp Psyllium husk powder (optional, for texture)
- 1/4 tsp Baking powder (optional)
- PUMPKIN CHAFFLES:
- 1/2 oz Cream cheese
- 1 large Egg
- 1/2 cup Mozzarella cheese (shredded)
- 2 tbsp Pumpkin puree
- 2 tbsp Besti Monk Fruit Allulose Blend
- 3 tsp Wholesome Yum Coconut Flour
- 1/2 tbsp Pumpkin pie spice
- 1/2 tsp Vanilla extract (optional)
- 1/4 tsp Baking powder (optional)
- SPICY JALAPENO POPPER CHAFFLES:
- 1 oz Cream cheese
- 1 large Egg
- 1 cup Cheddar cheese (shredded)
- 2 tbsp Bacon bits
- 1/2 tbsp Jalapenos
- 1/4 tsp Baking powder (optional)

Directions:

1. Preheat your mini waffle iron for about 5 minutes, until hot.

2. If the recipe contains cream cheese, place it into a bowl first. Heat it gently in the microwave (~15-30 seconds) or a double boiler, until it's soft and easy to stir.

3. Stir together all the chaffle batter ingredients (everything except toppings, if any), including the cream cheese from the previous step if the version you are making has it.

4. Pour enough of the chaffle batter into the waffle maker to cover the surface well. (That's about 1/2 cup batter for a regular waffle maker and 1/4 cup for a mini waffle maker.)

5. Cook until browned and crispy, about 3-4 minutes.

6. Carefully remove the chaffle from the waffle maker and set aside to crisp up more. (Cooling is important for texture!) Repeat with remaining batter, if any.

7. SPECIAL INSTRUCTION FOR CHURRO CHAFFLES ONLY:

8. Stir together Besti and cinnamon for topping. After the chaffles are cooked and no longer hot, brush them with melted butter, then sprinkle all over with the cinnamon "sugar" topping (or dip into the topping).

Peppermint Mocha Chaffles With Buttercream Frosting

Servings:6

Ingredients:

- Chaffles:
- 1 egg
- 1 ounce cream cheese at room temperature
- 1 tablespoon melted butter or coconut oil
- 1 tablespoon unsweetened cocoa powder or raw cacao
- 2 tablespoons powdered sweeteners
- 1 tablespoon almond flour
- 2 teaspoons coconut flour
- 1/4 teaspoon baking powder
- 1 teaspoon instant coffee granules
- 1/4 teaspoon vanilla extract
- Pinch salt
- Filling:
- 2 tablespoons butter at room temperature
- 2-3 tablespoons powdered sweeteners
- 1/4 teaspoon vanilla extract
- 1/8 teaspoon peppermint extract
- Optional garnish: sugar-free starlight mints

Directions:

1. For the Mocha Chaffles:
2. Heat mini Dash waffle iron until thoroughly hot.
3. Beat all chaffle ingredients together in a small bowl until smooth.
4. Add a heaping 2 tablespoons of batter to waffle iron and cook until done about 4 minutes.
5. Repeat to make 3 chaffles. Let cool on wire rack.
6. For the Buttercream Frosting:
7. In a small bowl with a hand mixer, beat the butter and sweetener until smooth.
8. Add the heavy cream and vanilla extract and beat at high speed for about 4 minutes, until light and fluffy.
9. Spread frosting on each chaffle and garnish with sugar-free starlight mints, if desired

Key Lime Pie Chaffle Recipe

Servings:2

Directions:

1. Preheat the mini waffle iron.
2. In a blender add all the chaffle ingredients and blend on high until the mixture is smooth and creamy.
3. Cook each chaffle about 3 to 4 minutes until it's golden brown.
4. While the chaffles are cooking make the frosting.
5. In a small bowl, combine all the ingredients for the frosting and mix it until it's smooth.
6. Allow the chaffles to completely cool before frosting them.

NOTES

Top with whipped cream or the cream cheese frosting. Add a small amount of lime zest for an extra touch!

Rice Krispie Treat Chaffle Copycat Recipe

Servings:2

Ingredients:

- Chaffle batter:
- 1 Large Egg room temp
- 2 oz. Cream Cheese softened
- 1/4 tsp Pure Vanilla Extract
- 2 tbs Lakanto Confectioners Sweetener
- 1 oz. Pork Rinds crushed
- 1 tsp Baking Powder
- Marshmallow Frosting:
- 1/4 c. Heavy Whipping Cream
- 1/4 tsp Pure Vanilla Extract
- 1 tbs Lakanto Confectioners Sweetener
- 1/2 tsp Xanthan Gum

Directions:

1. Plug in mini waffle maker to preheat.
2. In a medium mixing bowl- Add egg, cream cheese and vanilla.
3. Whisk until blended well.
4. Add sweetener, crushed pork rinds and baking powder.
5. Mix until well incorporated.
6. (optionallsprinkle extra crushed pork rinds onto waffle maker.
7. Then add about 1/4 scoop of batter over, sprinkle a bit more pork rinds.
8. Cook 3-4 minutes then remove and cool on a wire rack.
9. Repeat for remaining batter.
10. Make the Marshmallow Frosting:
11. Whip the HWC, vanilla and confectioners until thick and fluffy.
12. Slowly sprinkle over the xanthan gum and fold until well incorporated.
13. Spread frosting over chaffles and cut as desired, then refrigerate until set.
14. Enjoy cold or warm slightly in the microwave for 10 seconds.

Crispy Everything Bagel Chaffle Chips

Servings:1

Ingredients:

- 3 Tbs Parmesan Cheese shredded
- 1 tsp Everything Bagel Seasoning

Directions:

1. Preheat the mini waffle maker.
2. Place the Parmesan cheese on the griddle and allow it to bubble. About 3 minutes. Be sure to leave it long enough or else it won't turn crispy when it cools. Important step!
3. Sprinkle the melted cheese with about 1 teaspoon of Everything Bagel Seasoning. Leave the waffle iron open when it cooks!

4. Unplug the mini waffle maker and allow it to cool for a few minutes. This will allow the cheese to cool enough to bind together and get crispy.

5. After about 2 minutes of it cooling off, it will still be warm.

6. Use a mini spatula to peel the warm (but not hot cheese from the mini waffle iron.

7. Allow it to cool completely for crispy chips! These chips pack a powerful crunch which is something I tend to miss on Keto!

NOTES

The more cheese you use the thicker the chips will be. The less cheese you use the lighter and more crispy the chips will be! This technique works well for both textures! Just be sure to use less Everything Bagel seasonings if you use less cheese. You don't want the seasonings to be overpowering to the ratio of cheese you have.

This makes 6 chips and they will fill you up!

Chaffle Pizza

Servings:2

Cooking Time: 11 Minutes

Ingredients:

- FOR THE CHAFFLE:
- 1 large egg
- 1 teaspoon coconut flour
- ¼ teaspoon baking powder
- 1/2 cup finely shredded mozzarella

- TO ASSEMBLE:
- ¼ cup sugar free pizza sauce or marinara
- ¼ cup shredded mozzarella
- 6 slices pepperoni

Directions:

1. Plug in your mini waffle iron to preheat. Preheat oven to 425 degrees.

2. To make the chaffle crust, add the egg, coconut flour, and baking powder to a small bowl and whisk together with a fork.

3. Stir in the shredded cheese.

4. Spoon half of the batter into the waffle iron and spread carefully to the edges.

5. Close the waffle iron and cook for 3-4 minutes or until the waffle maker stops steaming.

6. Repeat with remaining batter.

7. To assemble, place the cooked chaffles on a small baking sheet.

8. Spread with the marinara, sprinkle with the mozzarella, and top with the pepperoni.

9. Bake for 5 minutes or until cheese is melted to your liking.

Notes

Feel free to adjust toppings to suit your tastes.

Peanut Butter Cup Chaffles

Servings:1

Cooking Time: 6 Minutes

Ingredients:

- FOR THE CHAFFLE:
- 1 large egg
- 2 tablespoons cocoa powder
- 1 tablespoon sweetener
- 1 tablespoon sugar freechocolate chips
- 1/4 teaspoon espresso powder
- 1/2 cup finely shredded mozzarella
- FOR THE PEANUT BUTTER FILLING:
- 3 tablespoons creamy peanut butter
- 2 tablespoons powdered sweetener
- 1 tablespoon butter, softened

Directions:

1. TO MAKE THE CHAFFLES:
2. Plug in the waffle iron to preheat.
3. Whisk together the egg, cocoa powder, sweetener, chocolate chops, and espresso powder. Stir in the mozzarella.
4. Add half of the batter to the waffle maker and cook for 3 minutes. Repeat with remaining batter.
5. TO MAKE THE PEANUT BUTTER FILLING:
6. Add all of the ingredients to small bowl and stir together with a fork until smooth and creamy.
7. TO ASSEMBLE:
8. Let waffles cool before spreading with the peanut butter and closing to form a sandwich.

Notes

Please note that I've deducted sugar alcohols from this recipe as erythritol generally has no effect on blood sugar. If you count sugar alcohols in your carb count, you'll want to calculate this yourself.

Apple Pie Fries With Caramel Dipping Sauce Recipe

Servings:6

Ingredients:

- (Egg-Free) Fathead Pie Dough Ingredients:
- 1 cup mozzarella whole milk, shredded
- 1/2 cup almond flour superfine
- 1/2 T Swerve Confectioners
- 1 T cream cheese full fat
- 1/4 tsp glucomannan helps dough crisp
- Jicama "Apple" Pie Filling Ingredients:
- 1 cup jicama chopped small
- 2 T Swerve Brown
- 2 T butter
- 1/2 T apple pie spice
- 1/2 tsp apple extract
- 1/4 tsp vanilla extract
- 1 packet True Lemon
- Cinnamon Sugar Ingredients:
- 2 T Swerve Brown
- 1/2 tsp Ceylon Cinnamon
- Caramel Dipping Sauce Ingredients:
- 2 T butter

- 2 T Swerve Brown
- 1 T Swerve Confectioners
- 1/4 cup heavy cream
- 1/8 tsp xanthan gum
- 1/8 tsp kosher or sea salt
- 1 tbsp water

Directions:

1. (Egg-Free) Fathead Pie Dough
2. Place the mozzarella and cream cheese in a microwaveable bowl.
3. Microwave for 1 minute, stir and then cook for another 30 seconds.
4. Stir in sweetener, almond flour, and glucomannan.
5. Let the dough cool slightly, then knead until smooth.
6. Roll out dough between two pieces of parchment paper. The thinner you roll the dough the crispier your "fries" will be.
7. Cut out circles with 3-4 inch cookie cutter.
8. Take scraps and knead together. You may need to reheat slightly.
9. Continue cutting circles until all dough is used.
10. Jicama "Apple" Pie Filling
11. Combine chopped jicama with butter, sweetener, lemon packet and spices in a pan.
12. Cook and stir over medium heat until jicama has softened.
13. Remove from heat and add apple and vanilla extracts.
14. Let cool slightly before adding to a food processor. Pulse until filling is smooth.
15. Cinnamon Sugar
16. Preheat dash GRIDDLE.
17. Place one dough circle on the griddle.
18. Add 1-2 tsp of "apple" filling and top with another piece of dough.
19. Cook 3-4 minutes until golden.
20. Sprinkle with Cinnamon Sugar mixture generously on both sides of the pie immediately after removing from the dash griddle.
21. Place on a cooling rack.
22. When fully cooled (put in the fridge to speed up cooling) slice into fries!
23. Dip in your favorite caramel sauce or whipped cream and enjoy!
24. Caramel Dipping Sauce
25. Combine butter and sweeteners in a small saucepan.
26. Bring to a boil over medium heat and cook 3 to 5 minutes (careful not to burn it).
27. Remove from heat and add cream. The mixture will bubble vigorously.
28. Sprinkle with xanthan gum and whisk to combine.
29. Add salt.
30. Return mixture to heat and boil 1 more minute.
31. Let cool to lukewarm and stir in water until well combined.

NOTES

TIP: You can speed up the cooking process by microwaving the jicama with 1/2 cup of water for 5 minutes. Drain excess water and follow the above steps.

Pizza Chaffles

Servings:1

Cooking Time: 15 Minutes

Ingredients:

- Chaffle
- 1 large egg
- ½ cup freshly grated cheddar cheese (cheddar, mozzarella, or jack cheese are all fine)
- Pizza Toppings
- 1 to 2 tablespoons pizza sauce (use sugar free if following keto)
- ¼ cup mozzarella cheese
- 5 to 6 slices pepperoni (use bacon, ham, italian sausage, or other favorite)
- optional: any other favorite pizza toppings

Directions:

1. Preheat oven to broil (or an air fryer to 400 degrees F). Also, preheat waffle maker to the highest setting.
2. In a small bowl add shredded mozzarella cheese, egg, and Italian seasoning. Mix well.
3. Pour mixture over the center of the hot waffle maker and close lid. Cook until the outside is to your desired crispiness.

4. Top with pizza sauce, then mozzarella, then pepperoni.
5. Transfer to a baking sheet or an air fryer basket. Broil or cook in an air fryer until cheese is melted and bubbly. Be careful not to burn!

NOTES

Don't miss all of our helpful hints, substitution ideas, cooking tips

VARIATIONS: Use any favorite pizza topping.

NOTE: if using a mini waffle iron this recipe will make 2 chaffles. If using a standard waffle iron, this will make one.

Savory Chaffle

Ingredients:

- 8 oz Monterrey Jack cheese8 oz Monterrey Jack cheese
- 3 eggs3 eggs
- 6 tablespoons almond flour6 tablespoons almond flour
- 1 ½ teaspoons baking powder1 ½ teaspoons baking powder
- 1 tbsp heavy whipping cream1 tbsp heavy whipping cream
- 1/4 tsp Chili flakes (optional)1/4 tsp Chili flakes (optional)
- 1/8 tsp Salt1/8 tsp Salt
- 1/4 tsp Italian seasoning¼ tsp Italian seasoning

- You can use any spices or seasonings of your choiceYou can use any spices or seasonings of your choice

Directions:

1. Whisk the first 5 ingredients until well blended

2. Add the spices and/or seasonings and blend well

3. Spoon about 1 ½ tablespoons of batter into mini waffle iron

4. Cook until golden brown and crispy

Notes

My waffle maker is a 4in Mini made by Dash. I got it from Kohl's.

Krispy Kreme Copycat Of The Glazed Raspberry Jelly-filled Donut

Ingredients:

- Krispy Kreme Copycat Donut Chaffle Ingredients:
- 1 egg
- 1/4 cup mozzarella cheese shredded
- 2 T cream cheese softened
- 1 T sweetener
- 1 T almond flour
- 1/2 tsp Baking Powder
- 20 drops glazed donut flavoring
- Raspberry Jelly Filling Ingredients:
- 1/4 cup raspberries
- 1 tsp chia seeds
- 1 tsp confectioners sweetener
- Donut Glaze Ingredients:
- 1 tsp powdered sweetener
- A few drops of water or heavy whipping cream

Directions:

1. Make the chaffles:

2. Mix everything together to make the chaffles first.

3. Cook them for about 2 1/2-3 minutes.

4. Make the Raspberry Jelly Filling:

5. Mix together in a small pot on medium heat.

6. Gently mash raspberries.

7. Let cool.

8. Add between the layers of Chaffles.

9. Make the Donut Glaze:

10. Stir together in a small dish.

11. Drizzle on top Chaffle.

Pumpkin Spice Chaffles

Servings:3

Cooking Time: 12 Minutes

Ingredients:

- 1 cup of mozzarella cheese
- 2 tablespoons almond flour
- 1 tsp baking powder
- 2 eggs
- 1/2 tsp pumpkin pie spice
- 2 tsp of Swerve

Directions:

1. In a small bowl mix the eggs, almond flour, mozzarella cheese, baking powder, pumpkin pie spice and swerve.

2. Once it is mixed well pour into a small food processor and blend until smooth.

3. Pour 1/3 of the batter into your mini waffle maker and cook for 3-4 minutes. Then cook the more of the batter to make a second chaffle and continue on until all pumpkin spice chaffles are made.

4. Serve with Low carb syrup and butter or a sprinkle of swerve confectioners sweetener!

Carnivore Chaffle Recipe

Servings:1

Cooking Time: 8 Minutes

Ingredients:

- 1/4 cup pork panko crushed pork rinds
- 1/4 cup parmesan cheese grated
- 1 tsp GrillMates Roasted Garlic & Herb seasoning
- 1 egg beaten

Directions:

1. Combine all the ingredients in a small bowl and mix until fully combined.

2. Using a small baking sheet, layer it with parchment paper or a silicone mat.

3. Pat the mixture into a small circle with wet hands or use a silicone spatula to shape the pizza crust.

4. Oven baking time: Bake at 350 degrees in oven for 10 minutes on each side.

5. Mini Dash Waffle maker: Divide the batter into 2 and cook each portion for a minimum of 4 minutes until it forms a crust (longer if you are using a large waffle iron)

6. Air fryer baking time: Bake at 300 degrees for 8 minutes on each side.

7. Remove the carnivore pizza crust and put keto friendly sauce of choice on with any toppings you choose. She used cooked Italian sausage and black olives

8. Top with 1/3 c mozzarella cheese.

9. Put back in the oven, air fryer or microwave just long enough to melt the cheese until it's golden brown. The oven or air fryer might take 3 to 4 minutes and the microwave may only take 1 minute.

NOTES

This recipe only has 1 net carb because of the sauce! This can be consumed with a small salad as a side! It's very filling and tastes amazing!!!

SWEET CHAFFLE RECIPES

Pumpkin Pie Chaffle

Servings:1

Cooking Time: 6 Minutes

Ingredients:

- 1 tbsp Pumpkin puree (from can)
- 1/4 tsp Pumpkin Pie Spice
- 1 tsp Monkfruit sweetener
- 1 Tbsp Almond flour
- 1 Egg Whisked
- 1/3 cup Mozzarella
- Whipped Cream (optional)

Directions:

1. Preheat your mini waffle maker.

2. Whisk the egg then add everything except for the mozzarella. After everything is mixed well, add the mozzarella.

3. Cook 1/2 of the batter on the mini waffle iron for 2-3 minutes. Allow to cool on a wire rack, this will allow it to firm and crisp.

4. Cook the other half of the batter.

5. (optional) Top with whipped cream or your desired toppings (crushed pecans would be great).

Notes

Allow the chaffle to cool on a wire rack, this will allow it to crisp up.

Pumpkin Chaffle With Cream Cheese Frosting Recipe

Servings:4

Ingredients:

- 1 egg
- 1/2 cup mozzarella cheese
- 1/2 tsp pumpkin pie spice
- 1 tbs pumpkin solid packed with no sugar added
- Optional Cream Cheese Frosting Ingredients:
- 2 tbs cream cheese softened and room temperature
- 2 tbs monkfruit confectioners blend or any of your favorite keto-friendly sweetener
- 1/2 tsp clear vanilla extract

Directions:

1. Preheat the mini waffle maker.

2. In a small bowl, whip the egg.

3. Add the cheese, pumpkin pie spice, and the pumpkin.

4. Mix well.

5. Add 1/2 of the mixture to the mini waffle maker and cook it for at least 3 to 4 minutes until it's golden brown.

6. While the chaffle is cooking, add all of the cream cheese frosting ingredients in a bowl and mix it until it's smooth and creamy.

7. Add the cream cheese frosting to the hot chaffle and serve it immediately.

Chocolate Chip Chaffles

Servings:2

Cooking Time: 6 Minutes

Ingredients:

- 1 large egg
- 1 teaspoon coconut flour
- 1 teaspoon monkfruit sweetener
- 1/2 teaspoon vanilla extract
- 1/2 cup finely shredded mozzarella
- 2 tablespoons sugar-free chocolate chips

Directions:

1. Plug in your waffle iron to preheat.
2. Add the egg, coconut flour, sweetener, and vanilla to a small bowl and whisk together with a fork.
3. Stir in the shredded cheese.
4. Spoon half of the batter into the waffle iron and dot with half of the chocolate chips. Spread a bit of batter over each chocolate chip.
5. Close the waffle iron and cook for 3-4 minutes or until as crisp as you'd like.
6. Repeat with remaining batter.
7. Serve hot with whipped cream or low carb ice cream.

Notes

I prefer Lakanto Monkfruit Sweetener as it's all-natural and doesn't have any aftertaste. Feel free to use whatever sweetener you prefer.

Cream Cheese Chaffles

Servings:2

Cooking Time: 8 Minutes

Ingredients:

- 2 tsp Coconut Flour
- 4 tsp Sweetener sugar alternative or preferred sweetener
- 1/4 tsp Baking Powder
- 1 Whole Egg room temp
- 1 oz Cream Cheese room temp
- 1/2 tsp Vanilla Extract

Directions:

1. Gather all the ingredients. Note - For quick room temperature eggs, submerge egg in warm water for 3-5 min. For quick room temperature cream cheese, take needed amount and microwave for 10-15 sec.
2. Pre-heat waffle iron.
3. In a small mixing bowl, add Coconut Flour, sweetener, baking powder and mix.
4. Next, add egg, cream cheese, vanilla extract and mix with a whisk until well combined.
5. Pour batter into waffle iron and cook for 3-4 min until browned to liking. Enjoy with your favorite waffle toppings.

Coconut Chocolate Chip Macadamia Nut Chaffles

Servings:3

Cooking Time: 9 Minutes

Ingredients:

- 1 tbsp Coconut Flour
- 1/2 Cup Roasted Macadamia Nuts
- 2 tbsp Sweetener sugar alternative or preferred sweetener
- 1/2 tsp Baking Powder
- 2 Egg room temp
- 2 oz Cream Cheese room temp
- 1 tsp Vanilla Extract
- 1 tbsp Low Carb Chocolate Chips

Directions:

1. Gather all the ingredients. Note – For quick room temperature eggs, submerge the egg in warm water for 3-5 min. For quick room temperature cream cheese, take the amount needed and microwave for 10-15 sec.
2. Plug-in Dash Mini Waffle Maker to pre-heat.
3. In a high powered blender, add in Coconut Flour, Roasted Macadamia Nuts, sweetener, Baking Powder and mix on high until combined. Take a spatula and scrape off the sides from the blender.
4. Now combine egg, cream cheese and Vanilla Extract into the blender. Mix at high speed for 10-20 seconds until a smooth batter is attained.
5. Pour batter into waffle iron, top with 5-10 Low Carb Chocolate Chips and cook for 3-4 min until browned to liking. Enjoy with your favorite sugar-free syrup or as is!

Blueberry Chaffles

Servings:2

Cooking Time: 6 Minutes

Ingredients:

- 1 tbsp Coconut Flour
- 4 tsp Sweetener sugar alternative or preferred sweetener
- 1/4 tsp Baking Powder
- 1 Egg room temp
- 1 oz Cream Cheese room temp
- 1/2 tsp Vanilla Extract
- 1/4 Cup Blueberries

Directions:

1. Gather all the ingredients. Note – For quick room temperature eggs, submerge egg in warm water for 3-5 min. For quick room temperature cream cheese, take amount needed and microwave for 10-15 sec.
2. Plug-in Dash Mini Waffle Maker to pre-heat.
3. In a small mixing bowl, add Coconut Flour, sweetener, baking powder and mix.
4. Next, add egg, cream cheese, vanilla extract and mix with a whisk until well combined.

5. Pour batter into waffle iron, top with 4-5 fresh blueberries and cook for 3-4 min until browned to liking. Enjoy with your favorite sugar-free syrup.

Grilled Cheese Chaffle

Servings:1

Cooking Time: 10 Minutes

Ingredients:

- 1 egg
- 1/4 teaspoon garlic powder
- 1/2 cup shredded cheddar
- 2 Slices American cheese or 1/4 cup of shredded cheese
- 1 tablespoon butter

Directions:

1. Heat up your dash mini waffle maker.
2. In a small bowl mix the egg, garlic powder and shredded cheddar cheese.
3. Once the dash waffle maker is heated up add in half the chaffle mixture. Cook for 4 minutes and remove.
4. Add the remainder of the chaffle mixture to the dash mini waffle maker and cook for 4 minutes.
5. Once both chaffles are done heat a pan on the stove over medium heat.
6. Add 1 tablespoon butter and melt it. Once the butter is melted in the pan and place 1 chaffle down in the pan. Top that chaffle with the cheese of your choice and add the second chaffle on top of it.
7. Heat the chaffle for 1 minute on the first side and flip over and cook for another 1-2 minutes on the other side to finish melting the cheese.
8. Once the cheese is melted remove from the pan and enjoy!

Mcgriddle Chaffles

Servings:2

Cooking Time: 7 Minutes

Ingredients:

- 3/4 cup Shredded Mozzarella
- 1 Egg
- 1 tbsp Sugar-Free Flavored Maple Syrup we used Choc Zero Maple Syrup
- 1 tbsp Sweetener sugar alternative or preferred sweetener
- 1 Sausage Patty
- 1 Slice American Cheese

Directions:

1. Gather all the ingredients.
2. Plug-in Dash Mini Waffle Maker to pre-heat.
3. In a small mixing bowl, beat egg.
4. Next, add shredded Mozzaerlla, sweetener, Choc Zero Maple Syrup and mix with a whisk until well combined.
5. Place ~2 tbsp of egg mix onto the Dash Mini Waffle Maker, close lid and cook for 3 - 4 minutes. Repeat for as many waffles you are making.

6. Meanwhile, follow cooking instructions for sausage patty and place cheese onto patty while still warm to melt.

7. Assemble Chaffle McGriddle and enjoy!

Pumpkin Chocolate Chip Chaffles

Servings:3

Cooking Time: 12 Minutes

Ingredients:

- 1/2 cup shredded mozzarella cheese
- 4 teaspoons pumpkin puree
- 1 egg
- 2 tablespoons granulated swerve
- 1/4 tsp pumpkin pie spice
- 4 teaspoons sugar free chocolate chips
- 1 tablespoon almond flour

Directions:

1. Plug in your waffle maker.

2. In a small bowl mix the pumpkin puree and egg. Make sure you mix it well so all the pumpkin is mixed with the egg.

3. Next add in the mozzarella cheese, almond flour, swerve and pumpkin spice and mix well.

4. Then add in your sugar free chocolate chips

5. Add half the keto pumpkin pie Chaffle mix to the Dish Mini waffle maker at a time. Cook chaffle batter in the waffle maker for 4 minutes.

6. DO NOT open before the 4 minutes is up. It is VERY important that you do not open the waffle maker before the 4 minute mark. After that you can open it to check it and make sure it is cooked all the way, but with these chaffles keeping the lid closed the whole time is VERY important.

7. When the first one is completely done cooking cook the second one.

8. Enjoy with some swerve confectioners sweetener or whipped cream on top.

Chocolate Chip Chaffles

Servings:2

Cooking Time: 8 Minutes

Ingredients:

- 1/2 cup shredded mozzarella cheese
- 1 tbsp almond flour
- 1 eggs
- 1/4 tsp cinnamon
- 1/2 tbsp Granulated Swerve
- 2 tablespoon low carb chocolate chips like Lily's chocolate chips

Directions:

1. Plug in your waffle maker.

2. In a small bowl mix the mozzarella cheese, almond flour, egg, cinnamon, swerve and chocolate chips.

3. Add half the keto chocolate chip Chaffle batter to the Dish Mini waffle maker at a time. Cook chaffle batter in the waffle maker for 4 minutes.

4. When the first one is completely done cooking cook the second one.

5. Let each chaffle sit for 1-2 minutes on a plate to firm up. Enjoy alone , sprinkled with powdered sugar or whipped cream on top.

Easy Double Chocolate Chaffles Recipe

Servings:1

Cooking Time: 4 Minutes

Ingredients:

- Double Chocolate Chaffles
- 1 eggs - medium
- 1/2 cup pre-shredded/grated mozzarella
- 1 tbsp granulated sweetener of choice or more to your taste
- 1 tsp vanilla extract
- 2 tbsp almond meal/flour
- 1 tbsp sugar-free chocolate chips or cacao nibs
- 2 tbsp cocoa powder (unsweetened) unsweetened
- 1 tsp heavy whipping cream

Directions:

1. Combine the ingredients for your chosen flavour in a bowl.
2. Preheat your waffle maker. When it is hot, spray with olive oil and pour half the batter into the mini-waffle maker (or the entire batter into a large waffle maker).
3. Cook for 2-4 minutes then remove and repeat.
4. Top, serve and enjoy.

Strawberry Shortcake Chaffle

Cooking Time: 12 Minutes

Ingredients:

- 3 Strawberries
- 1/4 cup Keto Whipped Cream
- 1/2 tablespoon granulated swerve
- 1 tablespoon Almond flour
- 1 egg
- 1/2 cup mozzarella cheese
- 1/4 teaspoon vanilla extract

Directions:

1. Heat up your waffle maker.
2. Rinse and chop up your fresh strawberries. Place the strawberries in a small bowl and add 1/2 tablespoon granulated swerve. Mix the strawberries with the swerve and set aside.
3. In a bowl mix the almond flour, egg, mozzarella cheese, granulated swerve and vanilla extract.
4. Pour 1/3 of the batter into your mini waffle maker and cook for 3-4 minutes. Then cook another 1/3 of the batter and the rest of the batter to make 3 keto chaffles.
5. While your second chaffle is cooking, make your keto whipped cream if you do not have any on hand.
6. Assemble your Strawberry Shortcake Chaffle by placing whipped cream and strawberries on top of your sweet chaffle. Then drizzle the juice that will also be in the bowl with the strawberries on top.

Cream Cheese Chaffle With Lemon Curd

Servings:2-3

Cooking Time: 4 Minutes

Ingredients:

- one batch keto lemon curd (recipe here)
- 3 large eggs
- 4 ounces cream cheese, softened
- 1 tablespoon low carb sweetener (I use Lakanto Monkfruit)
- 1 teaspoon vanilla extract
- 3/4 cup mozzarella cheese, shredded
- 3 tablespoons coconut flour
- 1 teaspoon baking powder
- 1/3 teaspoon salt
- (optional) homemade keto whipped cream

Directions:

1. Prepare lemon curd according to instructions and let cool in the refrigerator.
2. Meanwhile, heat waffle maker and oil it as you normally would.
3. In a small bowl, add coconut flour, baking powder and salt. Mix well and set aside.
4. In a large bowl, add eggs, cream cheese, sweetener, and vanilla. Using a hand beater, beat until frothy. You may have chunks of cream cheese leftover and that is fine.
5. Add mozzarella cheese to the egg mixture and continue beating.
6. Add dry ingredients to egg mixture and continue mixing until well combined.
7. Pour batter into preheated waffle maker and cook it as you would a waffle. Often just a few minutes.
8. Remove from waffle maker, top with chilled lemon curd, optional whipped cream and serve.

BASIC CHAFFLE RECIPES

Easy Maple Iced Soft Gingerbread Cookies Chaffle Recipe

Servings:2

Ingredients:

- Chaffles Ingredients:
- 1 egg
- 1 ounce cream cheese softened to room temperature
- 2 teaspoons melted butter
- 1 tablespoon Swerve Brown sweetener
- 1 tablespoon almond flour
- 2 teaspoons coconut flour
- 1/4 teaspoon baking powder
- 3/4 teaspoon ground ginger
- 1/2 teaspoon ground cinnamon
- Generous dash ground nutmeg
- Generous dash ground clove
- Icing Ingredients:
- 2 tablespoons powdered sweeteners
- 1 1/2 teaspoons heavy cream
- 1/8 teaspoon maple extract
- Water as needed to thin the frosting

Directions:

1. Heat mini Dash waffle iron until thoroughly hot.
2. Beat all chaffle ingredients together in a small bowl until smooth.
3. Add a heaping 2 tablespoons of batter to waffle iron and cook until done about 4 minutes.
4. Repeat to make 2 chaffles. Let cool on wire rack.
5. Maple Icing Directions:
6. In a small bowl whisk together sweetener, heavy cream, and maple extract until smooth.
7. Add enough water to thin to a spreadable consistency. (I used about 1 teaspoon water.)
8. Spread icing on each chaffle and sprinkle with additional ground cinnamon, if desired.

Chicken Jalapeno Popper Chaffle Recipe

Servings:2

Ingredients:

- 1/2 cup canned chicken breast
- 1/4 cup cheddar cheese
- 1/8 cup parmesan cheese
- 1 egg
- 1 small jalapeno diced (fresh or pickled)
- 1/8 tsp onion powder
- 1/8 tsp garlic powder
- 1 tsp cream cheese room temperature

Directions:

1. Preheat the mini waffle maker.
2. In a medium-size bowl, add all the ingredients and mix until it's fully incorporated.

3. Pour half of the mixture in the mini waffle maker and cook it for a minimum of 4 to 5 minutes.

NOTES

Optional Toppings: sour cream, ranch dressing, hot sauce, cilantro, green onion, feta cheese, or jalapeno!

Bacon Cheddar Bay Biscuits Chaffle Recipe

Servings:6

Ingredients:

- 1/2 cup Almond Flour
- 1/4 cup Oat Fiber
- 3 strips of Bacon cooked and crumbled
- 1 Egg beaten
- 1/4 cup Sour Cream
- 1 T Bacon Grease melted
- 1 1/2 T Kerrygold Butter melted
- 1/2 cup Sharp Cheddar Cheese shredded
- 1/2 cup Smoked Gouda Cheese shredded
- 1/4 tsp Swerve Confectioners
- 1/2 tsp Garlic Salt
- 1/2 tsp Onion Powder
- 1/2 T Parsley dried
- 1/2 T Baking Powder
- 1/4 tsp Baking Soda

Directions:

1. Preheat mini waffle maker.

2. Mix almond flour, baking powder, baking soda, onion powder and garlic salt to a bowl and mix using a whisk.

3. In another bowl, add the eggs, bacon, sour cream, parsley, bacon grease, melted butter and cheese. Mix until combined.

4. Add the dry ingredients into the wet and mix.

5. Scoop 2-3 T of the mix into hot waffle iron and cook for 5-6 minutes.

Low-carb Chocolate Chip Vanilla Chaffles Recipe

Servings:1

Cooking Time: 4 Minutes

Ingredients:

- 1/2 cup pre-shredded/grated mozzarella
- 1 eggs - medium
- 1 tbsp granulated sweetener of choice or more to your taste
- 1 tsp vanilla extract
- 2 tbsp almond meal/flour
- 1 tbsp sugar-free chocolate chips or cacao nibs

Directions:

1. Combine the ingredients in a bowl.

2. Preheat the mini waffle maker. When it is hot spray with olive oil and pour half the batter into the waffle maker. Cook for 2-4 minutes then remove and repeat.

3. Top, serve, and enjoy.

Arby's Chaffle

Servings:1

Cooking Time: 10 Minutes

Ingredients:

- FOR THE BEEF:
- 1/2 cup beef broth
- 4 ounces thin-sliced deli roast beef
- FOR THE CHAFFLE BUN:
- 1 egg, beaten
- 1 teaspoon coconut flour
- 1/4 teaspoon baking powder
- 1/2 cup finely shredded mozzarella
- FOR THE LOW CARB ARBY'S SAUCE:
- 1 tablespoon sugar-free ketchup
- 2 teaspoons Italian salad dressing
- 1/4 teaspoon Worcestershire sauce
- 1/4 teaspoon cracked pepper

Directions:

1. FOR THE BEEF:
2. Add the beef broth to a skillet and bring to a simmer. Add the beef and cook on low for 5 minutes to warm beef through. Cover and set aside while preparing the chaffle.
3. FOR THE CHAFFLE:
4. Plug in the waffle iron to preheat.
5. Whisk together the egg, coconut flour, and baking powder. Stir in the mozzarella to combine.
6. Spoon half of the batter into the waffle iron. Close the waffle maker and cook for 3 minutes. Remove the waffle and repeat with remaining batter.
7. FOR THE ARBY'S SAUCE:
8. To prepare the Arby's sauce, whisk together all of the ingredients.
9. TO ASSEMBLE:
10. Place the beef over one of the chaffles and drizzle with the Arby's sauce. Top with the second chaffle.
11. Serve immediately.

Notes

Add my keto cheese sauce to make this a beef and cheddar!

Sprinkle the chaffles with minced dried onion while cooking for an onion bun.

If you're an Arby's sauce fiend, you'll want to double the sauce recipe!

Buffalo Chicken Chaffle Recipe For Low Carb Waffles

Servings:2

Cooking Time: 4 Minutes

Ingredients:

- ¼ cup almond flour
- 1 teaspoon baking powder
- 2 large eggs
- ½ cup chicken, shredded
- ¼ cup mozzarella cheese, shredded

- ¼ cup Frank's Red Hot Sauce + optional 1 tablespoon for topping
- ¾ cup sharp cheddar cheese, shredded
- ¼ cup feta cheese, crumbled
- ¼ cup celery, diced

Directions:

1. In a small mixing bowl, whisk the baking powder into the almond flour and set aside.
2. Preheat waffle maker to medium/high heat and spray generously with low carb non-stick spray.
3. In a large bowl, add eggs and beat until frothy.
4. First, add in hot sauce and beat until well combined.
5. Add flour mixture to eggs and mix until just combined
6. Finally, add in shredded cheeses and mix until well combined.
7. Fold in shredded chicken.
8. Add chaffle batter to preheated waffle maker and cook until browning on the outside. About 4 minutes.
9. Remove from waffle maker and repeat Step 7 until all batter is used up.
10. Plate chaffles and top with feta, celery, and/or hot sauce and serve.

Low Carb Bagel

Servings:2

Cooking Time: 6 Minutes

Ingredients:

- 1 large egg
- 1 teaspoon coconut flour
- 1 teaspoon Everything Bagel seasoning (plus more, for serving)
- 1/2 cup finely shredded mozzarella cheese
- 2 tablespoons cream cheese, for serving

Directions:

1. Plug in your mini waffle iron to preheat.
2. Whisk together the egg, coconut flour, and bagel seasoning until well combined. Stir in the cheese.
3. Spread half of the egg mixture into the waffle iron and cook for 3 minutes.
4. Remove the waffle and repeat with the remaining egg mixture.
5. Spread each bagel waffle with cream cheese and sprinkle with additional bagel seasoning, as desired.

Notes

Use a sharp knife to cut a whole from the center of the waffle to make it feel more like a bagel or just eat it as is!

Jalapeno Popper Chaffles

Servings:2

Ingredients:

- 1 egg
- 1 tbsp almond flour
- 1/2 cup shredded cheddar cheese (plus more for the griddle)
- 1 tbsp softened cream cheese
- 1/2 tbsp freshly diced jalapeno
- 2 tbsp crumbled bacon
- pinch garlic powder

Directions:

1. Preheat your mini waffle maker.
2. In a small bowl, whisk the egg together and then add the rest of the ingredients and mix well.
3. Sprinkle a little shredded cheddar directly onto the griddle.
4. Pour half of the batter in and sprinkle with a little more cheese.
5. Close the lid and cook for 3-5 minutes or until the automatic timer or light goes off; repeat for next chaffle.
6. Enjoy alone or with a little cream cheese spread over top!

Sloppy Joe Chaffle Recipe

Servings:4

Ingredients:

- Sloppy Joe Ingredients:
- 1 lb ground beef
- 1 tsp onion powder you can substitute for 1/4 cup real onion
- 1 tsp garlic minced
- 3 tbs tomato paste
- 1/2 tsp salt
- 1/4 tsp pepper
- 1 tbs chili powder
- 1 tsp cocoa powder this is optional but highly recommended! It intensifies the flavor!
- 1/2 cup bone broth beef flavor usually
- 1 tsp coconut aminos or soy sauce if you prefer
- 1 tsp mustard powder
- 1 tsp Swerve brown or Sukrin golden
- 1/2 tsp paprika
- Cornbread Chaffle Ingredients:
- Makes 2 chaffles
- 1 egg
- 1/2 cup cheddar cheese
- 5 slices jalapeno diced very small (can be pickled or fresh)
- 1 tsp Franks Red Hot Sauce
- 1/4 tsp corn extract optional but tastes like real cornbread!

- Pinch salt

Directions:

1. Cook the ground beef with salt and pepper first.
2. Add all the remaining ingredients.
3. Allow the mixture to simmer while you make the chaffles.
4. Preheat waffle maker.
5. In a small bowl, whip the egg.
6. Add the remaining ingredients.
7. Spray the waffle maker with nonstick cooking spray.
8. Divide mixture in half.
9. Cook half the mixture for about 4 minutes or until golden brown.
10. For a crispy outer crust on the chaffle, add 1 tsp cheese to the waffle maker for 30 seconds before adding the mixture.
11. Pour the warm sloppy joe mix onto a hot chaffle and voila! Dinner is served!!

Hot Ham & Cheese Chaffles

Servings:2

Cooking Time: 6 Minutes

Ingredients:

- 1 large egg
- 1/2 cup shredded swiss cheese
- 1/4 cup chopped deli ham
- 1/4 teaspoon garlic salt
- 1 tablespoon mayonnaise
- 2 teaspoons dijon mustard

Directions:

1. Plug in your waffle iron to preheat.
2. Whisk the egg in a small bowl. Stir in the cheese, ham, and garlic salt to combine.
3. Spoon half of the mixture into the hot waffle iron, close, and cook for 3-4 minutes or until your waffle iron stops steaming and the waffle is cooked through.
4. Remove the waffle to a plate and repeat with the remaining batter.
5. Stir together the mayo and mustard to use as a dip.
6. Slice the waffles in halves or quarters and serve with the dip.

Notes

You may use any cheese you prefer.

This recipe yields 2 waffles. I'd recommend eating 2 as an easy lunch or 1 as a snack.

Easy Blueberry Chaffle Recipe

Servings:2

Ingredients:

- 1 egg
- 3 tbs almond flour
- 1 tbs cream cheese
- 1/4 tsp baking powder
- 5 or 6 blueberries
- 1 tsp blueberry extract optional

Directions:

1. Preheat waffle maker.

2. In a small bowl, whip the egg.

3. Add the remaining ingredients.

4. Spray the waffle maker with nonstick cooking spray.

5. Divide mixture in half.

6. Cook half the mixture for about 3 to 4 minutes or until golden brown.

7. Top with these possible options: dust with monkfruit, more blueberries, whipped cream, frosting, or just eat it plain!

NOTES

Optional Glaze: 1 tbs cream cheese warmed in the microwave for 15 seconds, 1/4 tsp strawberry extract, and 1 tbs monkfruit confectioners blend.

Mix and spread over the warm chaffle.

Optional Cream Cheese Frosting: 1 tbs cream cheese (room temp), 1/4 tsp blueberry extract, 1 tbs room temp butter (room temp), and 1 tbs monkfruit confectioners blend. Mix all ingredients together and spread on top of the chaffle.

You can also top it with simple whipped cream and blueberries.

Homemade whipped cream: 1 cup heavy whipping cream, 1 tsp vanilla, 1 tbs monkfruit confectioners blend. Whip until it forms peaks. Easy peasy!

Low Carb Sourdough Copycat Wonder Bread Chaffle Recipe

Servings:2

Ingredients:

- 1 egg

- 1 tablespoon almond flour

- 1 tablespoon mayo

- 1/8 teaspoon baking powder

- 1 teaspoon water

- 10 drops sourdough flavoring

Directions:

1. Mix ingredients together.

2. Cook in a Dash Mini Waffle Maker or sandwich maker.

3. Assemble sandwich with your favorite meat, cheese, and veggies.

Basic Low Carb And Keto Chaffle

Servings:1

Cooking Time: 5 Minutes

Ingredients:

- 1 large egg

- ½ cup freshly grated cheddar cheese (cheddar, mozzarella, or jack cheese are all fine)

Directions:

1. Preheat waffle iron to the highest setting.

2. In a small bowl add egg and grated cheese. Mix well until combined.

3. Pour mixture over the center of the hot waffle maker and close lid.

4. Cook until the outside is to your desired crispiness.

NOTES

Don't miss all of our helpful hints, substitution ideas, cooking tips!

VARIATIONS: use any variety of shredded cheese, add dried herbs, chopped chives, and red pepper flakes if you like spice.

SERVING SUGGESTIONS: Use as a bun for sandwiches, sloppy joes, tacos, burgers, hot dogs, and brats.

NOTE: if using a mini waffle iron this recipe will make 2 chaffles. If using a standard waffle iron, this will make one.

Oreo Cookie Chaffle Recipe

Servings:3

Ingredients:

- Chaffle Ingredients:
- 1 egg
- 1 tbs black cocoa
- 1 tbs monkfruit confectioners blend or your favorite keto-approved sweetener
- 1/4 tsp baking powder
- 2 tbs cream cheese room temperature and softened
- 1 tbs mayonnaise
- 1/4 tsp instant coffee powder not liquid
- pinch salt

- 1 tsp vanilla
- Frosting Ingredients:
- 2 Tbs monkfruit confectioners
- 2 Tbs cream cheese softened and room temp
- 1/4 tsp clear vanilla

Directions:

1. In a small bowl, whip up the egg.

2. Add the remaining ingredients and mix well until the batter is smooth and creamy.

3. Divide the batter into 3 and pour each in a mini waffle maker and cook it for 2 1/2 to 3 minutes until it's fully cooked.

4. In a separate small bowl, add the sweetener, cream cheese, and vanilla. Mix the frosting until everything is well incorporated.

5. Spread the frosting on the waffle cake after it has completely cooled down to room temperature.

Monte Cristo Chaffle Crepes Recipe

Servings:3

Ingredients:

- 1 egg
- 1 T almond flour
- 1/4 tsp vanilla extract
- 1/2 T Swerve Confectioners
- 1 T cream cheese softened
- 1 tsp heavy cream
- Pinch of cinnamon

Directions:

1. Mix all ingredients in a small blender.

2. Let batter rest for 5 minutes.

3. Pour 1 1/2 Tablespoons of batter in preheated dash griddle.

4. Cook 30 seconds.

5. Flip with tongs and cook a few more seconds.

6. Place 1 slice of cheese, 1 slice of ham and 1 slice of turkey on each crepe.

7. If desired, microwave for a few seconds to slightly melt the cheese.

8. Roll the crepes with the filling on the inside.

9. Serve the filled crepes sprinkled with Swerve Confectioners and drizzled with low carb raspberry jam.

Pumpkin Chaffles

Servings:4

Cooking Time: 12 Minutes

Ingredients:

- 2 large eggs
- ¼ cup pumpkin puree
- 2 teaspoons pumpkin pie spice
- 2 teaspoons coconut flour
- ½ teaspoon vanilla
- 1 cup finely shredded mozzarella cheese

Directions:

1. Plug in waffle maker to preheat. Spray with non-stick spray.

2. Add the eggs, pumpkin puree, pumpkin pie spice, coconut flour, and vanilla to a small bowl and whisk well to combine.

3. Stir in the cheese.

4. Spoon 1/4 of the batter into the hot waffle iron and smooth the batter out to the edges of the waffle iron.

5. Close the iron and cook for 3 minutes.

6. Remove the waffle and set aside. Repeat with remaining batter.

7. Serve hot with butter and sugar free syrup, as desired.

Notes

Add 1-2 teaspoons of sweetener to the batter, if you prefer a sweeter waffle.

Lupin Flour Waffle Recipe

Ingredients:

- Sweet Lupin Waffle
- 1 Tbs Lupin Flour
- 1 Tbs Monkfruit Confectioners
- 1 Egg
- 1 Tbs heavy whipping cream
- 1/4 tsp baking powder
- Savory Lupin Waffle
- 1 Tbs Lupin Flour
- 1 tsp Tabasco sauce my favorite is the Smoked Tabasco Sauce here
- 1 Egg

- 1 tsp water
- 1/4 tsp baking powder

Directions:

1. Preheat the mini waffle maker.

2. In a small bowl, whip the egg.

3. Add the remaining ingredients and mix until it's well incorporated.

4. Let the mixture sit for about 2 minutes as it will start to thicken a bit.

5. Pour 1/2 the mixture into the waffle maker. The mixture may seem very watery but don't worry, it will make the perfect waffle!

6. Cook it for exactly 2 minutes.

NOTES

Note: The reason I used monkfruit sweetener in this recipe is that the lupin can be kind of bitter. This combination comes out perfect with no bitterness at all. Top with optional keto sugar free syrup, butter, sugar free chocolate chips, or anything else you desire!

Zucchini Chaffles

Servings:2

Cooking Time: 5 Minutes

Ingredients:

- 1 cup Zucchini grated
- 1 Eggs beaten
- 1/2 cup shredded parmesan cheese
- 1/4 cup shredded mozzarella cheese
- 1 teaspoon Dried Basil or 1/4 cup fresh basil, chopped
- 3/4 teaspoon Kosher Salt divided
- 1/2 teaspoon Ground Black Pepper

Directions:

1. Sprinkle about 1/4 teaspoon of salt on the zucchini and let it sit while you gather your ingredients. Just before using, wrap the zucchini in a paper towel, and press to squeeze out all the excess water.

2. In a small bowl, beat the egg. Add in grated zucchini, mozzarella, basil, 1/2 teaspoon salt, and pepper.

3. Sprinkle 1-2 tablespoons of shredded parmesan to cover the bottom of the waffle iron.

4. Spread 1/4 of the zucchini mixture. Top with another 1-2 tablespoons of shredded parmesan and close the lid. Use enough to cover the surface. Watch the video to see how.

5. Allow the zucchini chaffle to cook for 4-8 minutes depending on the size of your waffle maker. Typically, when the chaffle has stopped emitting clouds of steam, it is almost done. For best results, allow it to cook until well browned.

6. Remove and repeat for the next waffle(s).

7. Makes 2 full-size chaffles or 4 small chaffles in the Dash Mini.

8. Don't overfill! Use a max of 1/4 cup of the chaffle mixture in the Dash Mini at one time.

9. These freeze well. Freeze them, and then re-heat them in the toaster or your air fryer to re-gain crispiness.

10. Use these to eat alone with some butter, or as a sandwich bread alternative.

Jamaican Jerk Chicken Chaffle

Servings:4

Ingredients:

- Jamaican Jerk Chicken Filling
- 1 pound organic ground chicken browned or roasted leftover chicken finely chopped
- 2 tablespoons Kerrygold butter
- 1/2 medium onion chopped
- 1 teaspoon granulated garlic
- 1 teaspoon dried thyme
- 1/8 teaspoon black pepper
- 2 teaspoon dried parsley
- 1 teaspoon salt
- 2 teaspoon Walker's Wood Jerk Seasoning Hot and Spicy jar type paste
- 1/2 cup chicken broth
- Chaffle Ingredients:
- 1/2 cup mozzarella cheese
- 1 tablespoon butter melted
- 1 egg well beaten
- 2 tablespoon almond flour
- 1/4 teaspoon baking powder
- 1/4 teaspoon turmeric
- A pinch of xanthan gum
- A pinch of salt
- A pinch of garlic powder
- A pinch of onion powder

Directions:

1. In a medium saucepan, cook onion in the butter.
2. Add all spices and herbs. Saute until fragrant.
3. Add chicken.
4. Stir in chicken broth.
5. Cook on low for 10 minutes.
6. Raise temperature to medium-high and reduce liquid until none is left in the bottom of the pan.
7. Enjoy!

Basic Chaffle Recipe

Servings:2

Cooking Time: 6 Minutes

Ingredients:

- 1 large egg
- 1/2 cup finely shredded mozzarella

Directions:

1. Plug in the waffle maker to heat.
2. Crack the egg into a small bowl and whisk with a fork. Add the mozzarella and stir to combine.
3. Spray the waffle iron with non-stick spray.
4. Pour half of the egg mixture into the heated waffle iron and cook for 2-3 minutes.
5. Remove waffle carefully and cook remaining batter.
6. Serve warm with butter and sugar-free syrup.

Notes

This is the BASIC chaffle recipe and nothing more is needed, however adding 1 teaspoon of coconut flour or almond flour + 1/4 teaspoon of baking powder will give these a better texture.

For a breakfast chaffle, try adding a splash of vanilla or a dash of cinnamon. You may also add sweetener directly to the batter if you'd like.

We highly recommend mozzarella cheese for a basic chaffle as it has the most neutral flavor (it won't taste cheesy!). If you're making a savory chaffle and want that cheesy flavor, you can use cheddar or any other type of shredded cheese you like.

Buffalo Chicken Chaffle Recipe

Servings:6

Ingredients:

- 1 Can Valley Fresh Organic Canned Chicken Breast (5 ounces)
- 2 T Red Hot Wing Sauce
- 2 oz Cream Cheese softened
- 4 T Cheddar Cheese shredded
- 2 T Almond Flour
- 1 T Nutritional Yeast
- 1/2 tsp Baking Powder
- 1 Egg Yolk Can Use whole egg if no allergy
- 1 Flax Egg 1 T ground flaxseed, 3 T water
- *1/4-1/2 Cup Extra Cheese for the waffle iron

Directions:

1. Make flax egg and set aside to rest.

2. Drain liquid from the canned chicken. Mix all the ingredients together. Sprinkle a little cheese on the waffle iron. Let it set for a few seconds before adding 3 T of chicken mixture. (I used a large cookie scooThen add a little more cheese before closing waffle iron. Cook for 5 minutes.

3. Don't open the waffle iron before the time is up or you will have a mess. Remove and let cool before adding a drizzle of hot sauce and ranch dressing.

Chaffles Benedict

Servings:4

Cooking Time: 10 Minutes

Ingredients:

- For the Hollandaise Sauce
- 3 large egg yolks
- 1 tbsp lemon juice
- 2 pinches Kosher salt
- 1/4 tsp dijon mustard or hot sauce optional
- 1 stick (1/2 cup) salted butter
- For the Chaffles Benedict
- 12 large eggs divided
- 1 cup shredded cheddar
- 8 slices Canadian bacon

Directions:

1. For the Hollandaise Sauce

2. Put the egg yolks, lemon juice, salt, and optional dijon mustard or hot sauce into the bottom of the cup that came with your immersion blender.

3. Melt the butter in a separate container in the microwave, then allow it to cool for a couple of minutes. Pour the butter over the egg yolks.

4. Put the head of the immersion blender in the bottom of the cup and pulse it. You should see the bottom of the mixture begin to become cloudy and pale yellow. As you continue to pulse, the cloudy layer should begin to rise up to the surface. Gently rock and lift the head of the blender as you continue to pulse. Eventually, when the mixture is mostly emulsified, you can lift the head of the blender all the way to the surface to finish the sauce. It should be thick and creamy with no chunks, and should easily coat a spoon without running.

5. For the Chaffles

6. Heat up the waffle iron. Pour water in the bottom of your egg poacher pan and put it over medium-high heat.

7. Beat 4 of the eggs in a small bowl. Reserve the remaining eggs for poaching.

8. Sprinkle a tablespoon of cheese onto the bottom of the hot waffle iron. Add about a tablespoon and a half of the beaten eggs, being careful not to overfill, then sprinkle another tablespoon of cheese on top. Close the waffle iron and cook for about 2-3 minutes, until golden brown. Remove the waffle and repeat for all remaining egg and cheese. You should end up with 8 chaffles. Keep the finished ones in the oven on warm.

9. Fry the Canadian bacon in a frying pan, heat in the microwave, or heat two at a time in the waffle iron.

10. To poach the eggs, crack them directly into the cups and cook until the exterior is just set, about 4 minutes. Remove from heat. To assemble, place a slice of Canadian bacon on each chaffle, then top with a poached egg and Hollandaise. Sprinkle with pepper and serve immediately.

11. Macros per serving: 601 calories, 1 gram net carbs, 34 grams protein, 51 grams fat.

Easy Chicken Parmesan Chaffle Recipe

Ingredients:

- Chaffle Ingredients:
- 1/2 cup canned chicken breast
- 1/4 cup cheddar cheese
- 1/8 cup parmesan cheese
- 1 egg
- 1 tsp Italian seasoning
- 1/8 tsp garlic powder
- 1 tsp cream cheese room temperature
- Topping Ingredients:
- 2 slices of provolone cheese
- 1 tbs sugar free pizza sauce

Directions:

1. Preheat the mini waffle maker.

2. In a medium-size bowl, add all the ingredients and mix until it's fully incorporated.

3. Add a teaspoon of shredded cheese to the waffle iron for 30 seconds before adding the mixture. This will create the best crust and make it easier to take this heavy chaffle out of the waffle maker when it's done.

4. Pour half of the mixture in the mini waffle maker and cook it for a minimum of 4 to 5 minutes.

5. Repeat the above steps to cook the second Chicken Parmesan Chaffle.

NOTES

Top with a sugar free pizza sauce and one slice of provolone cheese. I like to sprinkle the top with even more Italian Seasoning too!

Broccoli And Cheese Chaffle

Servings:2

Cooking Time: 8 Minutes

Ingredients:

- 1/2 cup cheddar cheese
- 1/4 cup fresh chopped broccoli
- 1 egg
- 1/4 teaspoon garlic powder
- 1 tablespoon almond flour

Directions:

1. In a bowl mix almond flour, cheddar cheese, egg and garlic powder. I find it easiest to mix everything using a fork.

2. Add half the Broccoli and Cheese Chaffle batter to the Dish Mini waffle maker at a time. Cook chaffle batter in the waffle maker for 4 minutes.

3. Let each chaffle sit for 1-2 minutes on a plate to firm up. Enjoy alone or dipping in sour cream or ranch dressing.

Made in United States
Troutdale, OR
11/05/2023